The Event Planner's Essential Guide To Balloons

By
Sandi Masori, CBA, CMT

ISBN-13: 978-1494822835
ISBN-10: 1494822830

Table of Contents

Acknowledgements

There are so many people who contributed to this book. I'm going to try to list them (in no particular order).

My balloon mastermind group, who supplied me with the stories and photos that make up this book. They are listed in the next section and in the appendix, so for the sake of brevity I won't list all their names here.

The planners, who so graciously let me interview them. They are also listed in the next section.

My friends who helped edit and organize my thoughts, especially Rachel Porter, Aisulu Gates and John Finley.

Thank you to Marsha Gallagher and Janice Volpe.

My mentors and coaches; Clint Arthur, Mike Keonigs, Ed Rush, and CJ Matthews.

Last, but certainly not least; My editor/ dad, my babysitter/ mom, my husband, who took on prepping all of our jobs so I could travel for TV appearances and work on this book, and my amazing kids, who have been pondering the question of "do we actually have a mom?".

There are so many others who have helped,

Thank you all for your help, guidance, inspiration, patience and wisdom. Without you, I could not have written this book.

Photo and Design by Sandi Masori

Forward

Do you think that balloons are just for kids' parties or low-end events? When you think of balloons do you think 3 balloons on a weight? If so then this book is for you. If not, this book is still for you. This book is written for professional event planners, and non professionals who plan events. In this book you will learn what is really available from the balloon world- there have been so many advances and such a huge range of options. Balloons can take many different shapes, sizes and feels. And the plain fact is, balloons make people happy. They touch something deep inside of us that brings out our inner child. Very few media elicit the kind of response that balloons can. Through the photos and interviews in this book, you will learn about how to use balloons most effectively for various events, and how to get the most out of your balloon artist.

Photo and Design by Sandi Masori

About Sandi

People always ask me how I got started in balloons. I started my journey with balloons back in the early 90's when I was a teacher. It started out that I was cocktailing at a magic-themed dinner theatre to earn extra money to support my teaching habit. Eventually I started learning magic to keep up with what my new friends were talking about. One of the magician's wives had been a balloon artist, and she taught me my first few balloons designs. In the beginning, I just thought that it would be something fun to do in my classroom. Then she and I started busking in the bars and nightclubs around Los Angeles. Eventually my school went on break, and I was invited to perform in Japan. I spent the next few years traveling around the world, performing with balloons. After living in Japan for a year, I decided to move to Israel.

A couple of very significant things happened there, the first was that I met my husband, and the second was that I attended a workshop on decorating with balloons. Up to that point I was only focused on the entertainment side of the balloon industry, "twisting" as we call it. About a week after I took that workshop, we got a call to decorate a Bar Mitzvah. And so began the deco side of the business. When my husband and I got engaged, we came to San Diego to visit my family and my husband looked around and said "let's live here". So we moved back to San Diego, and in 2000 we opened Balloon Utopia. While still in Israel, I started teaching others how to do twisting balloons. After we moved back to San Diego I found myself often being requested to teach at industry conferences and conventions, initially teaching twisting balloons, and then later decor as well.

In 2009 I started studying marketing in order to make sure that Balloon Utopia kept up with the times, especially online. I found that marketing, especially online marketing and lead generation/ management was something that I really liked and was really excited about. Like most balloon companies, mine spent a lot of time trying to be everything for everyone. But as I got deeper into marketing, I realized that I enjoyed the corporate events most of all, and that the marketing systems I had been learning were a perfect tie in to the type of décor I was doing. Not every event needs the lead generation system, but for many events, especially conferences, trade shows and grand openings, the real reason that people are using balloons is to attract attention, get more leads, and ultimately make more money. Now, though I still do various events for which I am contracted, I spend most of my own marketing time and resources on the corporate market- both marketing to them and taking classes and workshops to better serve them.

In 2012 I wrote my first book *The Ultimate Guide To Inflating Your TradeShow Profits... With Balloons*. It hit the #1 best-seller spot on Amazon 3 times. In the fall of 2013 I gained the attention of the media, and started going around the country doing TV appearances on local and national shows, talking about balloons. The media gave me the title of "America's Top Balloon Expert", which I am greatly honored by. I even appeared on The Today Show! That was so much fun! I wrote a second book, designed to be an e-book for the media appearances called *25 Ways To Decorate Your Party Without Helium*. Somewhere along the line, my You Tube channel also racked up over 1,000,000 views.

I am passionate about always stretching myself to learn and grow. I love being a resource for people both on balloons and marketing, and especially on the point where they connect.

This book was so much fun to write. I was amazed at both the similarities and differences in the responses of all the balloon pros that I interviewed. The insight that the planners brought helped crystallize some of the ideas that I had been operating on, and really helped highlight the issues that matter most to you, the event planners.

Introduction

Though the media has been calling me "America's Top Balloon Expert", the truth is that I am inspired and blessed to be associated with many talented balloon artists and designers. We have an incredible industry that shares openly with each other. Through conventions, seminars, workshops, videos and online forums, we inspire and help each other.

In this book I have interviewed 9 other balloon artists to whom I look up to and regularly take inspiration from. I am lucky enough not only to call these people friends, but to share a professional association with them through our mastermind group. In fact, I would even go so far as to say that when clients come to me with pictures of balloons that they found on the internet, chances are really good that one of these nine are the original artist. All of us do many types of events, so even though I've tried to narrow it down by asking each of them to focus on one or two types of events, they are all equally skilled in any type of event.

In addition to these extraordinary designers, I've also interviewed several event planners. Some I have had the pleasure of working with and others I have only met online via event forums.

Before I introduce you to my contributors, I want to take just a moment to tell you how to use this book. You don't have to read this from start to finish, rather feel free to jump into whichever topic seems most timely and interesting for you at the moment.

The chapter on our favorite events is full of pictures, so feel free to browse through there for inspiration and amazement.

To make it easier, I'm going to put a short bio of each of the balloon artists here in alphabetical order, and in the appendix you will find a more complete bio of each of them.

Photo and Design by Sandi Masori

Photo and Design by Sandi Masori

Photo and Design by Sandi Masori

The Balloon Professionals

Anne McGovern

Anne McGovern, CBA from Elegant Balloons in New York City is the queen of centerpieces. She has a distinct style that has won her many awards and captured the hearts and interest of not only the balloon industry but the Pinterest community as well. Her distinctive style has been copied by many in the industry. In fact, Anne's website is where I'm likely to go when I need centerpiece inspiration. The incredible thing is that she's only been doing balloons since 2007! She's no stranger to special events though, as her pre-balloon job was as a corporate event planner.

Blenda Berrier

Blenda Berrier, CBA, from Balloon and Event Construction Company in Northeast Florida has been in the balloon industry since 2001. Blenda has won several awards for her parade floats--in fact, every year that they entered a float in the parade they won either first place or best overall. Besides being a talented balloon artist, Blenda is a planner's dream. Most of her clients are planners and she really "gets it" when it comes to understanding how to work with planners and what they need.

Chris Potts

Chris Potts, CBA, of Balloon Masters in Buffalo, NY, finds himself traveling a lot for events. While he and his staff cover his local area, he finds that he attracts a lot of larger companies and planners who like what he does so much that they'll bring him out to wherever the event is just to have him on site. He's also a balloon artist's balloon artist. He is frequently requested to fly out across the country to help other balloon companies with their larger events. He's also a regular instructor at the conventions and willingly shares with the online balloon community. Chris is an "old-timer" in the industry, having started in 1993. He was one of the first 50 balloon professionals to earn his CBA (Certified Balloon Artist) designation.

Dianna Glandon

Dianna Glandon, CBA, from Knoxville, TN, started Above the Rest Balloons in 2006. She made a name for herself pretty much as soon as she started though, winning awards at a variety of balloon conventions shortly after becoming a professional balloon artist. Dianna is also an expert at fabric draping and frequently will integrate fabric into her offerings and designs. She is no stranger to the needs of special events, having spent more than 25 years planning events, conventions, and workshops. She is also a lifelong student and goes to numerous conventions and workshops pertaining to balloon and business education. This gives her a unique and well-rounded perspective. Other balloon artists, including myself, often call her for advice and a dose of her positive attitude.

Holland Muscio

Holland Muscio of Balloonacy in Atlanta, GA, is a corporate planner turned balloon artist. She was the group sales and marketing director for the Atlanta Symphony, and has been planning events since she was a teenager. In 2004 she and her husband purchased their balloon company from one of her vendors who was moving out of town. Since then the pictures of her incredible décor have made the rounds in both the professional balloon forums and publications and captured attention at the international balloon conventions. Having been on both sides of the business, she has a special insight and perspective on the needs of putting together an event. She often brings her "planner" hat to her consultations with both her direct and planner clients.

Jill Shortreed

Jill Shortreed, from Charleston Balloon Company in South Carolina is a veteran of the balloon industry. She started in the early 90s doing kids parties, and had several retail party stores. Both she and her husband Scott earned their CBA designations, making them one of only a handful of companies with 2 CBAs on staff. In 2013 they were named as a finalist for the small business of the year by The Charleston Metro Chamber of Commerce. They are regularly published in the industry magazines and have been winning many of the inter-industry photo competitions. Her photos have inspired many other balloon artists to offer similar designs to their clients.

Joette Giardina

Joette Giardina of Party People Celebration Company in central Florida has been doing balloons since 2001. She got into balloons after going to a party supply convention. She pretty much exploded onto the scene as soon as she started, winning several awards at the industry conventions. She was quickly added to the convention instructor roster and her classes have been very popular. She often combines fabric into her balloon offerings for a different look and feel.

Steve Jones

Steve Jones, of Balloon Designers out of Seattle, WA, wears many hats in the balloon industry. Besides offering full service balloon décor and entertainment, he also produces instructional videos for the industry and hosts one of the most anticipated bi-yearly balloon conventions. In addition to all that, he's also the president of his local ISES chapter. Steve first came to my attention in the late 90s when we both wrote columns for an online balloon forum. He is prolific and engaging as a writer and I would look forward to his columns each month. He has also racked up a serious portfolio of awards and accolades and has very quickly become one of the most recognized people in the industry.

Tammy Corzine

Tammy Corzine, of Celebrations in Ohio, is another veteran of the balloon industry, having started in 1990. She has won numerous competitions and awards, including 'Designer of the Year' in 2010. Her photos are used in the industry magazines and she teaches at the international conventions. In addition to doing full service décor, Tammy also has a retail location where she offers party supplies and cash and carry balloons. This combined experience gives her a unique perspective on trends in the private event world. Tammy was also a member of the education board for the IBA (International Balloon Association), an industry watchdog organization.

Balloon Design and Photo By Holland & Sean Muscio

The Planners

Julie Prater

Julie Prater is the vice president of events for Texas Creative- a full service communications firm out of Texas. Many of their clients are large national companies that are doing events across the country. They specialize in corporate events ranging from grand openings to open houses, to press conferences and everything in between. One of her largest clients is a national chain that frequently uses balloons for all their grand openings across the whole country, and counts on her to hire professionals who can deliver a unified look regardless of the location.

Jessie Schwartzburg

Jessie Schwartzburg of Jessie Schwartzburg Events and Consulting, out of San Diego, CA, specializes in multi-speaker events (large 2-3 day conferences with multiple speakers appearing on the stage). She does other types of events as well, but feels that 90% of her clients are those planning large conferences. She started in event planning with The Learning Annex, a huge conference and speaker organization. All of her events are videoed and either live- streamed or offered for purchase later, so she has a unique set of challenges and needs that her professionals need to understand and be able to work around.

Sherry Truhlar

Sherry Truhlar, from Red Apple Auctions, has a very unique niche, specializing in auctions and galas-- with a focus on helping her clients make more money. Prior to starting her company, she was the corporate events planner for GE. Sherry is based in the Washington DC area, but often finds herself traveling for events across the country.

Photo and Design by Sandi Masori

Perceptions and Myths

There are numerous "myths" or misconceptions about balloons and the balloon industry. Educating the public and disproving these myths is one of the challenges that the professionals of the industry face. Some of the biggest misconceptions about balloons are: balloons are cheap, balloons are just for kids, balloons are cheesy, balloons are a hazard to the environment, balloons are inappropriate for high- end events, dependent on helium and that their sum total is balloons on string or arches.

Let's talk about these one at a time, starting with the idea that balloons are cheap. While balloon décor may be less expensive for the same coverage than other media- they are not cheap. The labor and skill involved in knowing the right way to put things together, when to use which elements, how to make things stable these skills have value, and one should expect to pay accordingly. None-the-less, when compared to the same amount of coverage in flowers, fabric or lighting, balloons are a very budget friendly option.

"Just for kids"... in actuality, balloons can be made into any shape, likeness or color scheme. If they are used in colors that appeal to

Balloon Design and Photo By Blenda Berrier

children, like a 4 color combo of red, yellow, blue and green, and integrated with childhood themes, then they will have corresponding appeal. If they are used in contrasting color combinations, like black and silver or black and gold, then they will play much more elegantly. Integrate in some shiny texture, like foil balloons or lights and the effect is downright beautiful. Perfectly appropriate for a high end Black Tie event. One thing about balloons though, however they are used, they reach something deep inside of us and draw out emotion. Simply put, balloons make people happy. No matter how they're used they touch us and bring out smiles.

A similar misconception, but more dangerous, is that balloons are cheesy. I had a planner tell me that what she most often sees at events is 3 balloons tied to a weight-- or worse to the chairs. I can say with absolute certainty that no balloon professional would recommend tying the balloons to a chair- that is either by the client's insistence or a DIY-er. As for 3 balloons on a weight, the few times I've done that it was by the planner's request. I think that in some ways it's like a self- fulfilling prophecy. Every balloon professional who I have interviewed agreed that the clients who get the best work from them are the ones who will trust their professional advice and ask what they recommend rather than putting in an order for 3 balloons on a weight. Don't get me wrong, there are times that 3 balloons on a weight is in fact the best option, but make those 3 balloons 16" or 3' balloons and you get a totally different effect. The key is to know that there are options and when each one would be best.

Now let's talk about the environmental issue. Latex balloons are 100% bio-degradable. Foil balloons are not, nor is the ribbon that may be attached to the balloons, but latex balloons themselves biodegrade at the same rate as an oak leaf. Leave a balloon out on a window sill that gets lots of sunlight and you can see the bio-degradation process in action. And, since balloons are made from the sap of the rubber tree, in order to get more balloons, you have to plant more trees. Sounds pretty green to me.

Speaking of natural resources, let's talk a bit about helium. We'll go into more detail about the helium situation in another section, but I want to point out that most balloon professionals find that helium is only about 20% of their business. Most of the really cool things that we can do are air-filled. The great thing about air-filled décor is that not only do we have much more control over the details, the designs are also longer lasting. Using framing, we can get an accurate reproduction of anything. Huge branded walls, giant mascots or figures, eye-catching columns, anything really- and it will last for more than a week under the right conditions (indoors, moderate temperature). Another point for balloons!

Photo and Design by Chris Potts

So I think the real lesson here is that when you're dealing with a professional, a professional's going to suggest things that will fit with the tone, theme and ambience that you were trying to create. For *best* results, and you're going to hear this over and over again, for best results you should ask your Balloon professional "what do you recommend" instead of using him or her as an order taker. Balloon professionals may have ideas that are on the cutting-edge that you would not have thought about.

One of our balloon artists, Holland, was actually a planner before she became a balloon artist and what she relates that the first time that she hired balloons, she was surprised by the cost of balloon decor because she had expected balloons to be cheap. But when she saw the reaction that people had to the balloons it made her decide that it was totally worth it because "People really respond to balloons, they put a smile on people's faces and the truth is that even as we say that balloons are not for children necessarily, or are not just for children, it does touch something deep inside everyone and brings out the child. All of us know this, even if the balloons look highly elegant, even if the color scheme is highly elegant, to be able to reach deep into somebody's psyche, deep into their emotion, to bring out their inner child and instantly put a smile on the face and get them in the mood to participate in the event or the party, that is very powerful."

Photo and Design by Holland and Sean Muscio

Every balloon artist I interviewed agreed with Holland. Chris said "the idea that balloons are just for kids parties, that's not true anymore. When you start putting color schemes together you get a very elegant look with balloons, you just have to realize that if it's a formal gala- it's a black tie and the women are wearing gowns, balloons are appropriate. Balloons make people smile automatically and how could that ever be a bad thing? How can making people smile and interesting decor ever be inappropriate? So I think that they just have to give balloons a chance to see that everybody loves them"

Jill agrees with the notion that balloons are better for the budget than other types of decor for the same coverage, however she cautions, "it's not that balloons are cheap it's just that comparatively for the same coverage they can be less expensive giving you your biggest bang for your buck, no pun intended"

In regards to the misconception that all the balloon decor out there is just three balloons on a weight, or a spiral arch, Holland says "There's so much that can be done to make it more-- even little things, like a balloon curl at the end. You can make it so different and to me what's important is people need to realize that it's there's more than just a bunch of balloons on string."

Holland adds: "There is a balloon decor design for every situation. There's something out there that can fit the situation and will work with any setting. I really think there's something we can design that will make your event-- not detract from your event, but enhance it"

Photo and Design by Steve Jones

And Blenda says "when used properly there are 1 million things you can do with balloons. They can create that emotion, they come with a certain sculpture or certain design, they can bring your corporate colors into an area or an event, and they're a great resource to have at tradeshows. It's no longer just balloon on the string as it may have been years and years and years ago. Now the possibilities are absolutely endless. People are wearing them, I mean they change. That's probably the number one thing that people need to know, that you could build a house with balloons. You could probably do anything you wanted out of Balloons- the possibilities are endless"

Agreeing Anne said "Before I got started with balloons, I had no idea this world existed. I didn't have any idea how beautiful balloons can be, what you can do. I think people's concept is still three balloons on a foil weight. I wouldn't give you that, I would never. So when I have a client call me, and say 'I just want something simple;' I say, 'let me send you some pictures and price to show you the work we do, to show you the kind of work we do, and then see if you want to proceed.' I think there's a misconception that balloons can't be classy, or they're not elegant. And they sure can be, there are so many things you can do with it. I mean, some people say to me, wow; is that really balloons? And I say, 'yeah, those are balloons.' And they can be long lasting, and especially for corporations, they can be cost effective. I mean, we did a cancer ribbon that lasted a month in a health care facility."

Steve adds "the biggest piece of advice I would give is to ignore the stereotype. There is a prevalent feeling in the event world... that 'balloons are okay for certain things and not for other things.' And of course, when they say 'the other things,' they're talking about events with big budgets where they fear balloons don't really belong, because of the stereotypes."

Sherry, a planner specializing in auctions, had this to say when asked about the balloon stigma "I think that there's a lot of creative ways to utilize balloons, and I think that maybe there is an image out there ... that some people have a thought that it's a little kids' sort of thing, and certainly it can be. But I think like with a lot of things, even with auctions, people go in perhaps with a preconceived idea of what is, but then once you start to get a little scratch under the surface you realize wow, this goes a lot deeper than what even I realized; there's a lot more things there that we can take advantage of that I didn't even know existed.

"Certainly I see that... there's lots of ways to utilize balloons. There lots of different balloons out there, and it doesn't have to be for a seven year old's birthday party. It can be something that's very elegant and majestic, and lends an air or aura of sophistication to an event that just hasn't been done before.... Like Fantasy flowers... I've seen those as centerpieces, which looked really nice... if you're doing it over the course of four or five days at a convention, and you want to keep things looking fresh, fantasy flowers ain't a bad way to go."

Photo and Design by Sandi Masori

Jessie, a planner who specializes in large multi-speaker multi-day events, said of balloons: "I think they're great attention grabbers, what we found a lot is if we're doing an event at a huge venue, like a hotel that has lots going at once, the balloons catch the attention of other people at that hotel. So people are coming up, and we're getting free marketing where people are saying, what's going on? What is this? And then they're taking some of our marketing materials, so that's really great. And I just think it's just a memorable experience too.

"You don't go to a lot of seminars and multi-speaker events where there are balloons, so it is that something different- like wow, that's cool..." Jessie added, "It's just something that they remember and we find a lot too where the balloons are helping us get marketed down the line, because when people meet someone at the event, and they want to get a picture with them, or when the speaker comes off the stage and they want to get a picture with them, they do it in front of the balloons.

"We see a lot of people doing that- taking pictures either on the stage or by one of the balloon columns, because it makes for a cool picture, so our marketing's living on. Because it's getting posted then on Facebook or people's various social media channels, so it's cool because not only is it attention grabbing, but then it lives on as well."

Photo and Design by Sandi Masori

So I just think balloons are a lot of fun for the right event and can just do a lot not only at your event, but down the road. You'll see how cool it shows up in picture and in video, and how consistent your branding is. So for people not thinking about using balloons, I would say to reconsider and look at some of the events we've put on with balloons and just see how cool they photograph, it's really neat."

The bottom line is that balloons, when in the right hands, can transform time and space, create an ambiance, elicit emotion, direct traffic, be photo ops, and create pure elegance. The trick is to make sure that you're entrusting them to the right person- a real balloon professional. We'll talk in another section about how to find one of those.

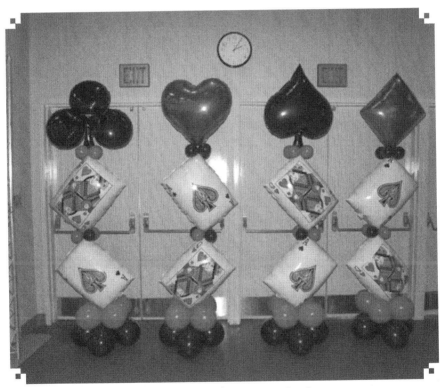

Photo and Design by Tammy Corzine

Photo and Design by Blenda Berrier

Photo and Design by Sandi Masori

Helium - what's the deal - why is the second most abundant element in the universe in such short supply?

The recent helium crisis is probably one of the most confusing things facing the balloon industry. I say confusing because the costs are rising, dramatically, and availability is limited. Many people either don't know about the helium shortage, or if they do know about it, they think that that means that there's also a balloon shortage. Most professional balloon companies find that helium is only 10-20% of what they do. Most of the décor they sell will be air-filled and framed in some way. Frames can be as simple as a baseplate and a pole to an elaborate 3-dimensional cage.

The big question though is if helium is the second most abundant element in the universe, why is there a shortage? While everyone knows that helium is used for party balloons, "floating" is only 3-11% of the total use of helium. The larger uses are for the medical and tech industries.

It's a perfect storm if you will. On the one hand, you have refineries in Europe and the Middle East that shut down for maintenance and have been closed longer than anticipated. On the other hand you have an increased demand for helium by the tech industry to manufacture flat screen TVs and touch screen devices. There are also the more widely known uses, cooling down MRIs, for example.

Because of the unique properties of helium, it is used for science, technology and medical uses. It's a noble gas, doesn't combine with any other gasses, is not flammable and has an extremely low freezing point.

Photo and Balloons by Sandi Masori

While all of this is happening we also have the fallout from a 1996 law passed by Congress called The Helium Privatization Act. Why would Congress care what happens with helium? Well, in the 1920s the United States created the Federal Helium Reserve to collect helium, which was then being explored for defense purposes. The federal helium reserve is the largest helium reserve in the world, and supplies 1/3 of the world's helium and over ½ of the helium used in the United States. This reserve was operating at a $1.4 billion deficit. So, in 1996 Congress passed the Helium Privatization Act, mandating that either by 2015, or by the time they paid off the $1.4 billion debt, the US government needed to get out of the helium business. So they started selling off the helium at below market rates. In October 2013 that debt was paid off, and we almost fell off the helium cliff. Even as the government was in the process of shutting down, they managed to pass the Helium Stewardship Act, which gave the US government one more year to sell helium at the same rates, but come 2015, that helium needs to be put up to auction and rationed off to the highest bidder. In the past two years, prices have increased over 500%, and I predict that come 2015 they will triple again.

In fact in an article in *Popular Science* in 2010, scientist Robert Richardson, was quoted as saying that party balloons should be $100 each. (http://www.popsci.com/science/article/2010-08/future-these-will-cost-100-each)

While we haven't quite gotten there, prices for helium filled party balloons vary greatly from one location to the next. There are still a ton of air-filled options though. In fact, air-filled décor is longer lasting than helium décor, and more customizable. There are many examples of air-filled décor in this book, and as a special gift, you can get a free copy of my e-book *25 Ways To Decorate Your Party Without Helium* by going to Http://www.BalloonUtopia.com/25Ways.

Photo and Design by Steve Jones

Photo and Design by Holland and Sean Muscio

How To Choose A Balloon Company - What separates the stars from the duds...

I asked both the pros and the planners what makes for a good balloon company, and how they would recommend going about finding one. I also asked what questions they thought planners should ask of their balloon people to make sure that they are getting the best one.

First the planners:

Julie: "We try to hire balloon partners who are certified, and y'all have a great network of industry leaders, we try to tap into that. I do my research online; I see who's certified. Looking at a website, or Facebook, social media, pictures will say a lot. See what the balloon partner is capable of doing, then we'll call. We just explain who we are, what we're doing, and what we're trying to do- we are very quick to say that we partner with many balloon artists across the country and what we want to do has been done, and here's a list of wonderful, top partners that we currently work with. If you have any questions, call them. And the balloon network is great; they do answer questions and give tips on how to make it happen successfully." *(Side note, we have an incredible network and can find you what you need in any major market).*

Jessie: "I would ask who they've worked with in the past, what their client list is. I would absolutely want to see pictures of past events. I think balloons are very visual things, so I'd want to see past examples, and I'd want to hear what their ideas are. A lot of time I would maybe just say, give something very raw, and say here are my colors, here's where I'm trying to go with this, what are your ideas? And then I like when a company can kind of visually take me through the process, so if they're like jump on my website, here's something I did that I would model it on, but maybe I'd make it fresh and new by doing this, or maybe they're kind of drawing it out for me. I'm visual, so I do like when people can kind of explain to me the end process of what it will look like."

Sherry: "Professionalism, reliability, price was part of it, but it's more important to make sure it works than it is to worry about price, because that's a function of value. The price was a function of those other things. So from that standpoint, particularly if you're around the world to attend a management meeting, it's not like you want to go cheap and have to explain on Monday why something didn't work."

Next let's see what the balloon pros had to say. Interestingly enough, the pros had a lot more to say about what you should look for.

Chris: "First do a little bit of leg work in just going through their website without even contacting them, and just seeing if they see some pictures that are like 'wow; that's really nice.' And then if it's the first time you're going to be using a decorator, you really should meet them face to face, and you can get a lot on first impressions. If you feel that this decorator is really qualified to do events, and is really going to provide what they say, that is great, and getting referrals is great. Call the hall that the event's going to be at, and say 'Have you worked with other balloon companies, and do you recommend anybody?' That's a great start also."

Joette: "Check out their website, but make sure that the work on it is theirs. If you think you've seen the same photo on multiple websites, ask them if it's theirs. In the balloon industry, a common mistake of new businesses is to use stock photos, or other people's pictures to put on their site. It's ok to be point blank with them and ask them, or ask for details about the event that the photo came from, if you're not sure."

Dianna: "When you look at their website, look at the quality of the pictures. Someone who is a professional is very precise, makes sure that the balloons are sized the way that they should be, the patterns are flawless, everything matches and complements each other. A good balloon professional should ask questions, not just take the order. They should want to know more about the event. Someone who's not a professional may not know they need to ask those kind of questions."

Anne: "Look at the work and see that everything is proportioned, even, and sized correctly. Make sure that they're insured. All professional companies carry insurance."

Holland: "Find out more about how they invest, have they done anything educationally, have they gone to any education series. Again, it's all investing; it could be as simple as what have you done to invest in your education and learning more about different products that you can offer me?"

Chris: "Find out the difference between air-filled décor and helium décor. A good balloon company probably does 90% air-filled décor on frames. Make sure that the decorator is familiar with the venue,

Balloon Design and Photo By Blenda Berrier

and if not, that they're going to take a good look at the venue, because you don't want to have a set up planned and then you get down there and there's a surprise about the ceiling type, or there's a surprise about how much room they have between the entrance and the first set of tables, or that in the foyer area, there's not the amount of room that you thought there was going to be. Then you would have to take décor, and instead of having it where you want it to be, where you envisioned it, they're having to squeeze it in somewhere else. So it's important to find a decorator who's very familiar with the venue."

Tammy: "Ask what we think will give the biggest impact, what's going to work best for your event. Hopefully they would trust our opinions because we've been doing this for a long time, and have been there, done that, so we know. Ask if the balloon artist has worked that venue before too. Ask what kind of events they've done, look at pictures. Ask how many events they have on a given day... is your event going to be the only one, or does the balloon artist have seven other events that day? If they do, ask how will they handle that and service all of them. "

Blenda: "They should know the right questions to ask, the balloon artist needs to be able to ask you the correct questions so they can give you a proposal that will fit the needs of your event, it's a matter of experience. For outdoor décor ask how they're going to weight it down, that they know how to weight it properly, that's probably the biggest disaster you could have for an outdoor event is wind and it doesn't take much for a balloon to blow   Ask them how early they will arrive, how much time they will need."

Jill: "Planners should ask 'what brand of balloons will be used'? Are you going to go to Party City and buying Party City balloons?' We're not. We are only going to use high quality, professional grade balloons whether that is Qualatex, or Betallic, or Anagram, or whomever. We're going to have an inventory in stock. We're going to be on time. You don't ever have to worry about us being late, with the exception of extenuating circumstances that some of us can never control. Do they have insurance and a business license? These are just basic business questions that should be asked of their caterer, florist and any other vendor. Any questions of credentials you would ask of any other professional company, I would ask of your balloon company."

Steve: "Ask the right questions, qualify them, and find out, I hate to say it, but the average balloon person isn't really that professional. I think that's one of the biggest reasons why the event world is so hesitant to use us. Ask really important questions. How long is this balloon going to float? Don't just assume that they're using a liquid additive to extend the float time, ask them. Ask questions, you know, throw information out there. Tell them we're having a screen, we're having this, we're having that. Wait to see what their response is. If they don't say anything about it or ask questions, maybe it's worth looking in another direction. It's really important to select the right person for the job. Don't just call random people, really investigate, Google them ,find out what their credentials are, find out what they can do, find out what their experience is and remember, longevity's not always the key."

I think that as everyone mentioned, the website is a good first step. After checking out the website, then you want to get an idea of their professionalism- you can find this out both by asking them questions and by paying attention to the questions that they ask you. If they just take your order, and don't try to make sure that you're getting the

Photo and Design by Joette Giardina

most appropriate décor for your event, you may want to keep looking. Though you may think that you know exactly what you want, if you give your balloon artist the chance to suggest what they think may work, you may be pleasantly surprised.

Photo and Design by Sandi Masori

Get The Most From Your Balloonies

I asked the planners what they wanted from their balloon artist, and here's what they had to say:

Jessie: "Attention to detail, like someone who's going to proof my work as well. I just love having people that are detail oriented, and just nice to work with, and people that I can tell want repeat business, where it's not just the one-time thing. To me, it's like the smartest vendors are the ones who realize that 'she has a thriving event business and it's not going to be just a one-off. I want to wow her this first time and then get hired back for all of her event instead of just the one time experience.' So that's what I'm looking for, and a lot of my vendors that I am loyal to, that's what they've done for me. I can tell they really care. They're double checking my work as well, and coming up with other ideas that maybe I haven't thought of. I love when people come up with creative ideas that I haven't thought of and they run it past me, I think that's really cool."

Julie: "I think it goes to what your client's goal is for the event, and for us, almost always with this one particular client it is about attention getting, so I'm a huge fan of balloons. I know they work, and I would say don't be afraid to use balloons and to trust your balloon artist in direction of what looks good and what's going to work. I know a lot of times we mandate they have to do this and then all of a sudden they come back to me and say, 'guess what, it's going to be too cold for foil balloons. You need to switch over to latex.' And it's like, 'oh yeah, thank you all right.' Just have those "plan Bs" in place, but also trust your balloon partner, because they are the professionals and they know all about balloons."

On the topic of how to work with your balloon pro, Jessie had this to say:

Jessie: "I prefer to say this is my budget, what can you do with it? It's easier for me, and that's just the way I work, with anything. It will be like my budget for décor is this, and out of that I can only take this much out for balloons, what can you do for me. And just find out what they can do and see if it would be a good fit."

When I flipped that question around, and asked the balloon pros what they wanted from a planner, here's what they had to say:

Chris: "I guess one that really sees the impact balloons have. I mean, I've done events with event planners where they want everything ballooned out, every single thing ballooned out, and I guess that's what you really want, somebody who can see that they're not buying balloons and latex per se; they're buying décor and the feeling that comes across with balloon décor, and when you make interesting arches, they're not balloons. It's just an interesting entrance piece. So I guess somebody who really just sees the impact and value that balloons have, and isn't afraid to try it for backdrops and arches at the entrance and just understands the feeling that all the guests get when they see balloon as opposed to plastic or wood panels."

Dianna: "The perfect planner is a person who is proactive and calls you well before one week before their event. They call you probably three or four months if not more before a large event. They have a budget in mind. They have some experience so that they know that the things they are doing while planning an event are not inexpensive. While balloons are very economical compared to other décor, things from a professional aren't cheap because you're paying for the service and the education. A pro would have a collaborative attitude of, 'Wow. Yes, let's consider this and that' and 'this idea would work' even though they may have had one idea in their head. Even a professional often doesn't know everything that a balloon artist can do. They have an open mind. They are willing to pay you your deposits or down payments that you ask. They pay on time. I think that's probably my perfect one. They are very organized, together, kind, all that stuff. Also tell us what story they want to tell, what kind of experience they want to create. So I don't know that they are asking us so much as they're just telling us in full what they want. I feel that is my job just to ask them. Being open minded is important. "

Photo and Design by Anne McGovern

Anne: "I understand there are budgets. I think the best thing to do for me, is when someone tells me what their budget is, exactly. Don't just shop around looking for an arch. You get the phone call, 'how much is an arch?' Well, what kind of arch? There are 50,000,000 kinds of arches. Does the arch have a theme? Is it air filled? Is it on a frame? I have a venue coming up in two weeks where that's what actually happened, somebody called and said 'I want an arch.' And then after I talked to them a little bit I found out that there's no helium allowed in this venue. There are so many arches, there's string of pearl arches, link-o-loon arches, garland arches... So I can't give you a price; I need to find out more information. So the more information I have about your client, about exactly what kind of a party it is, the better I can help you.

"That's the first thing I ask, the date, where the party is, what type of party it is, so you can figure out what they're looking for. Is it a 50th birthday? Is it a corporate event? How long do you need the décor to last? There's so many aspects that we need to know in order to give them a correct price. I think communication, budget, really explaining what their vision is, is going to get the results they want. Just because you tell me your budget is $2,000 it honestly does not mean I'm going to spend $2,000. I want to give you the vision of what you're going to do. If you tell me your budget is $5,000, you might only spend $4,500, I don't know.

"Sometimes I'll find if people tell me their budget they're going to get more out of me than trying to hide it, because I want to complete their vision. I want to give them a product that is going to make them so happy that they're going to come back for more. But if they're hiding it, and not telling me, or going around, or shopping around, it's just lack of communication."

Joette: "I think the main thing is just to find out exactly what's going on in the space, and how many people are going to be in it. Because I think sometimes we don't take into account how much room all the tables take up, or how much room the dance floor's going to need. And if you're putting some really cool canopy over the dance floor, you want to make sure that there's still plenty of room for the number of guests that are going to be there to dance and enjoy themselves."

Tammy: "The best planners to work with are those who know what they want as far as the impact and the overall appearance of the room, but will still allow some creativity on our part, because we know what's going to work best in a given situation, and to be a little bit flexible as long as we're getting the final impact that they want and the final atmosphere to the event. I think that's really important, because if they give us a definite 'I need three balloons on a weight', then what if we added some balloons curls to it or something to spice that up a little bit, and if they don't give them the freedom to do that and to maybe just design a little bit, then they may not get the best look for their money."

Holland: "Work as a team and communicate issues. We have one venue in town that requires that you have a parking pass in advance, and then we didn't know that till we got there, and then it delayed us 30 minutes in our installation. We could have been done with our installation by the time we got permission to actually park our vehicle, so it's those kinds of things that if we're all working together on making sure it's a good event, then it's better for everybody."

Jill: "I think the biggest thing with my planners and my marketing people is when we're getting all the information from you, and you're calling me to book your event, have all the information that we need. Just like the caterer and the florist would, I need the venue contact. We had this happen with a wedding a while back. The wedding planner told us to load in this particular area, but when we got to the facility we were told that's a non-loading zone. So we prefer to call the venue and confirm what their rules are ahead of time, or do they have any specific load-in instructions. If it's a venue we haven't done magnets in before, and we need to suspend something; are you okay with that? We do a have a few venues around here that can't have balloons in them. They mean helium balloons, but we need to clarify that with them. Is there another event beforehand? Another example would be when the bride told us us three weeks before that you can get in there at 8:00am, and we show up at 8:00am to start decorating, and there's still another event going on that they booked, a last minute event, and the bride didn't know about it. The biggest things are the who, what, when, where, why, and how, and give me the venue contact. And then just trust what we do; that's why you called us, for professional balloons, so why wouldn't you trust that we are professionals doing a professional job?"

Photo and Design by Jill Shortreed

I thought it was really interesting that though the ten of us are in very different locations, and run our businesses differently, every single balloon person that I interviewed said the planners who get the most out of them are the ones who will give the budget, the vision, the areas of interest, and then let the balloon person suggest what might work, as opposed to calling around price checking for the cheapest arch or column. Everyone agreed that when they know the budget they have to work with, they are going to suggest the very best décor for the event, venue and budget- and that the décor may or may not use the full budget. For me personally, I know that when I'm creating custom packages for my clients, my inner perfectionist takes over, and I'm likely to create a package with a much higher value than what the client pays, because that's what I think the event really needs. Sometimes when I'm creating these packages I'm able to take items that have a low profit margin and those that have a high profit margin, and put them together in order to make the budget.

The balloon pros also had more advice for planners on how to work most efficiently with their balloon person. They also shared some things that planners should take into consideration. The themes that came up ranged from knowing the venue, to volunteer labor, the various possibilities of balloons and other hidden considerations. One theme that was often mentioned was the way that balloons react in weather. Planner Julie also had some comments on this:

Julie: "We've learned a lot about balloons because we use them outside and weather can dictate the performance of a balloon. I appreciate all the education I have received from the balloon partners across the country, and the numerous phone calls educating me on balloons in order for me to educate my client on expectations. That's probably been the most difficult thing with balloons, which you wouldn't think. You think 'Hey, get some balloons and put them outside.' It's not that easy, because one day the client could see beautiful balloons in beautiful Florida, because it was a beautiful day, and then the next week that some person wonders why the foil balloon is shrinking and not performing and doesn't look so great. I think the expectation setting and the education for your client has been the most helpful thing we've found from working with balloon professionals."

Jill: "Balloons are a temporary product; they're not meant to last forever. Outside they will react differently than inside in a climate controlled area. Helium balloons are not going to work very well outside, and if they do it's for a short time. If you have balloons inside and outside, your outside balloons will look a little different than your inside balloons because of oxidation."

Tammy: "Set up times and tear down times, would have a big effect on what we can do. As does the environment inside, if it's temperature controlled or not. We have a lot of junior fair buildings that don't have air conditioning, so we're not going to do any helium stuff in there the night before. We're also going to be really selective on any air filled stuff we do the night before. Some of the places, with their fire suppression systems, have the lasers and if the balloons move, it'll set off alarms. So we need to know about any alarm systems."

The balloon pros also had other advice for planners on the various uses of balloons.

Photo and Design by Steve Jones

Joette: "A lot of times corporate event planners don't realize that they can take part of their signage budget and give that to the balloon professional. We can have custom balloons printed with the logo of the company that you're sponsoring. We can have signs that are directional signs with arrows put on them. It can be a really cool balloon sculpture or column put out rather than just your basic sign with an arrow. How creative, and how fun for your clients, to have something different as they're walking through the lobby to get them to their meeting, or to their special event, versus the basic chloroplast sign."

Chris: "I like to choose balloons over almost any other décor. I love fabric and lighting and ice carvings, but I think the event planners are really doing themselves and their clients a disservice, if they at least aren't familiar with what can be done with balloon décor; especially air filled balloon décor on frames, or suspended, or hung. The visual impact is just amazing, so I think that they really should get themselves familiar on what can be done. They don't have to go with balloons every time, but it's nice to know what their options are, and if they're on some sort of budget there is nothing out there that can get the visual impact like balloons. It's the best value. My favorite thing to work with."

Joette: "I think the number one thing with balloons is that it can be an art form, and so many people don't realize that unique and dynamic sculptures can made out of the balloons. Sometimes just adding a specialty item to a regular, standard balloon column will make their clients go 'wow!' as they walk in the door, and that is whole idea, taking something that people are not used to seeing in an artistic manner and putting it into that artistic spot that makes the event special. For corporate events, just seeing what a large scale sculpture can do for the backdrop, to create a really special space or a beautiful entrance. It's different than any other media, because it's not what people expect. It's not something everyone has seen. By calling a professional and talking to them about the event you're holding and asking, 'What would you think?' Give that balloon professional a chance to show you some photos of ideas that you may have never thought of."

Other themes covered were the amount of time it takes to set up and clean up, volunteer labor and safety considerations.

Dianna: "Challenges for corporate planners: How much time does the balloon artist have to actually install the décor? I think that is essential. If you have two days, or if you have two hours, that's a huge difference. The planner needs to know that the balloon artist needs to come in to see the venue. Even if you've seen it a hundred times, I think you should meet with them and actually look at the venue so they can talk to you about the overall design at the same time. I think they need to also consider things like how hard is the air condition-ing running inside the building, because it makes a difference. They need to consider line of sight for video screens, whether you're hang-ing from the ceiling, the layout of the room, how people are going to see, because it seems like people put these big tall centerpieces on the tables, and you can't see anything, and then they go on the floor."

Chris: "We've got a large staff and a lot of vehicles, so we do 90% of the inflating at our studio, and then we take it there all done. Ulti-

Photo and Design by Chris Potts

35

mately we would love to have four or five hours onsite to get set up. We want to come in as early as possible. We'd like to set up before the wait staff gets in there, so we can do our thing, pick a corner, do our set up, our constructing, and get things set up before the they start running around. I think the planners need to be aware that the balloons will last; if they're not a cheap helium balloon that's going to only stay inflated for a few hours. Most of our décor is air filled on frames, which will last days. Setting it up early is advantageous to us. If that's not possible, then we would bring four or five people and two or three vans."

Dianna: "A planner should think about how it's going to get cleaned up, and the impact that it has on the venue. It is my company policy that we go back clean up everything. It is an extra service, but we tell them this needs to be done, because they can't leave 'balloon guts' on the floor. They all need to be popped and cleaned up. If they want to bring it back to us, they are welcome to bring back all of the framing, the base plates, etc. If they want to fold the fabric they are welcome to fold the fabric. 95% of the time or more, they don't want to deal with it because as we tell them, 'You don't have to stay late. You don't have to come early. You don't have to get volunteers, and you don't have to worry about the cleanup.' Truthfully, with our venues, they love my company because we don't leave a mess, and that's really important to me. Sometimes it's a pain to go back late at night, so we may charge more for going back late at night. The venue does not like it if they have to clean up. A lot of venues, in their contract, will say that it is a 'no balloon' venue. Well, I'm allowed in 'no balloon' venues because I guarantee that nothing is going to the ceiling, and if it does I will get it down. I think that really relieves a lot of people's stress, or disappointment when they're told they can't use balloons."

On the topic of volunteers, and store bought balloons being added into the mix, Holland and Jill had this to say:

Holland: "As a planner you may be thinking of doing a balloon drop or balloons on ribbon and getting volunteers and doing it yourself. One thing you need to remember is that you can't always depend on using volunteers or even using the bar staff at the restaurant you're at. They're not always dependable. Also, their speed is so much slower, so it may end up taking longer, and therefore really cost more to have someone inexperienced do it. Quality and professionalism are important."

Jill: "We get a lot of customers who order all these beautiful balloons and décor from us, and then they run to the party store, or the dollar store, and buy cheap balloons on top of it. They bring them in, and they don't match the balloons that we have going on. So not only is there a color mismatch, but because they ran to the party store and picked up balloons, and didn't know anything about the properties of the balloons, their balloons don't last, or they start to explode because they were blown up in an air conditioned store, and then they were brought outside and left in 100 degrees in the blaring sun. Then they wonder why balloons start exploding all over the place. A professional will take heat related expansion, color choices and other conditions into account."

Photo and Design by Blenda Berrier

Steve and Tammy had some valuable advice on the general properties of balloons and helium.

Steve: "Event people need to understand that the gasses we work with are nonflammable. They are inert. Some people work with nitrogen, a lot with helium. The only danger involved is the tanks themselves, the pressure in the tanks. But, any responsible balloon person is going to keep them nice and secure as they work with them. They also always use valves and the proper equipment."

Tammy: "If you want clear balloons, you need to know that they're probably going to oxidize. We can balloon shine them, but that's going to cost more. "

Steve also had a lot to say about fire safety and considerations when it comes to balloons.

Steve: "It's important to know what the fire marshal's policies are in the building. It's import to think about balloon décor versus escape routes, because they have to be taken into account. Every once in a while, I'll get a planner who says 'just put that wall in front of the door.' I can't do that, that is a fire exit. There has to be a clear path to it, so that's something important to pay attention to."

Steve: "Something we ran into with Balloon Town was that we would create ceilings with balloons, and I mean full ceilings, complete and total ceilings. But, you have to allow sprinkler systems to come into the area, so if you do a canopy for example, you can't create that canopy to be air-tight, completely solid. There has to be room for water to come through. That's why a string of pearl canopy style, with the individual arches is fine, but a linking balloon canopy, a really tight one, may not be fire marshal approved. That's something to think about, a cross hatch, where it's an x pattern and there's big holes in between, that would be ok, because the water can pass through, but if you're like me and you want it nice clean and full, you can't do it as a ceiling structure."

On the topic of ceiling heights, Tammy had this to say:

Tammy: "Ceiling heights are really important. If the ceiling is only 8' high, and we do something on the ceiling, then we would just do a small cluster of balloons. For example, to hold up the dance floor, with swags of fabric or something like that. We usually do smaller arrangements on the tables because your space gets filled so quickly with such a low ceiling. With bigger ceiling venues we will usually do something taller, something bigger, maybe going from the 11 inch balloons to the 16 inch or 24 inch balloons. Of course, table size is going to dictate a lot too, because some of the venues have the banquet tables and some of them have big round tables, so that's going to dictate what you can do on them as well."

Photo and Design by Dianna Glandon

The balloon people that I interviewed also had some sage advice on why you would want to hire a balloon professional over a "weekend warrior" or part-timer. Here's what they had to say:

Steve: "This is the difference between an experienced professional and someone who does balloons, the reality is that the professionals understand not only what we can do, but why we need to do it. And sometimes there are situations where, you may think that you want something , but we may explain to you why it wouldn't work the way that you hope."

Anne: "I have insurance. That's another thing you have to make sure that the company you're hiring is reputable, that they have insurance, and that they can give them referrals."

Jill: "We had a company that price shopped, and they were going to hire us, but then at the last minute they decided to go with another company. They were doing multiple launches and had hired us for one and another company for the other. The other company was not a professional company and their arch snapped in the middle of the event. Before the event really even kicked off and got going, their arch was in two big wiggly lines. We had done the sister project on the harbor. Our stuff was fine, because we knew what we were doing. We recommended that they had to columns and not arches. We told them that we would stand behind what we did, that the columns were not going to topple over. Obviously we can't control poppage, but the décor was going to be installed safely, and they didn't have to worry about it. When we came back to pick it up later that day everything still looked great."

Anne: "I had a lady call me yesterday, and her balloon person canceled on her last minute for this weekend. I can't even imagine that anybody would do that to somebody. When I gave her my price, she said 'oh you're so much more expensive.' Well, you get what you pay for. I'm not going to cancel. I've never canceled in my life. I'd go sick as a dog if I had to."

Jill: "We just did the grand opening for the children's center, she did not give me a specific budget. We did have to tweak the décor a little bit, but she trusted what we came up with, which was doing a sculpture. She originally had just called us to do a balloon arch, and I recommended a sculpture instead, based on where everything was going to get installed, and offered to do their logo.

"We did flanking columns. We also did what we call event poles, which were stationed on the playground fence, all the way around. It was a marketing company that hired us. We actually get quite a bit of that, where we are hired by marketing companies that are focused on branding.

"We actually converted one of the companies that couldn't stand balloons. That's one of my best testimonials to this day. She didn't think that balloons and adults fit, and she couldn't believe that by the end of the night, they were fighting to take home the pieces. They've hired us multiple times since then."

Blenda: "When the production company gets really overwhelmed, when they've got too much work, they're going to start selling bal-

Photo and Design by Jill Shortreed

loons, because they know I'm going to do it, and it's something they don't even have to think about. It works for me, I know they have a lot of props and décor, but when they're thin and they can't do it, they're going to start selling balloons for that day because they know I'll take care of everything."

Photo and Design by Joette Giardina

Photo and Design by Chris Potts

Photo and Design by Steve Jones

Photo and Design by Sandi Masori

Photo and Design by Blenda Berrier

Do's And Don'ts

Though I'm going to attribute these do's and don'ts to the various people I interviewed, the truth is that the comments I got from all the balloon pros were so similar, that virtually any of them could have been attributed to any of us. I found it fascinating that though we are separated by geography, collectively we had all had very similar experiences while working with planners.

Do: Have an open mind. Let us help you figure out what you need to do. - Tammy

Do: Tell us what your budget is. That's a big one for us. People tend to be stingy with that information. A lot of times, I'll say "Do I have $50 or do I have $5000?" And usually they'll say "oh, I don't have $5000 but I have more than $50." So getting it narrowed down to a budget, that's really going to speed things along and make sure you're getting what you can afford and what's going to work for your event. – Tammy

Do: Know your venues and your restrictions and things like that. – Tammy

Do: Know what your client wants and how to translate it back to me, so I know how to translate that vision into balloons- Tammy

Don't: Use me as an order taker, when you tell me your budget and vision, and let me suggest what to do, you're going to get much better décor from me because I may suggest things that you wouldn't have thought of. ' Sandi

Do: Feed your balloon artists a vendor meal if other vendors are getting one. Our crews are often the first ones in and the last ones out. We work hard to make your event perfect and should be granted the same respect and perks as any other vendor – Sandi

Do: Know what the weather will be and plan your balloons accordingly. Tammy says, "A lot of people want to do outdoor parties in the summer in Ohio, and it's usually not conducive to balloons because the weather's so unpredictable. Right now, it's in the 70's and it's pouring down rain. Yesterday, it was about 60 degrees and windy. Tomorrow, it may be in the 90s and hot and humid, so it's hard to plan outdoor décor in this area." In general, when planning outdoor décor you want to assume that it will be windy and hot and plan accordingly.

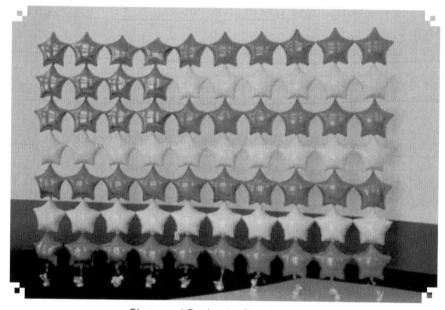

Photo and Design by Blenda Berrier

Do: Take ceiling height into consideration. "Some of the venues in the area, they may only have an eight or nine foot ceiling. Some of the others have twenty to thirty foot ceilings, so you really need to take that into consideration with the impact that you're going to have with décor." Tammy

Don't: Ask for a donation for a non-profit event. "Every single non-profit event asks for a donation. And certain times of the year are huge non-profit times. All the fun runs are going on, all the bike rides, all the charity walks.... Every single one of them starts out the conversation with 'Can you donate to our cause?' And as much as I would like to, we can't. At the end of the day many balloon companies are mom and pop businesses that work very hard and put in very long hours. We're not deep pocketed organizations like McDonalds. Please understand that a company may not be able to give it away, but may be able to work with you in other ways..." – Steve. *(Note from Sandi: Often, if you ask, the balloon company has a non-profit discount that they can give you, or if you give them the budget, they can figure out the best custom package for your money and your needs. The other thing is that if you establish a relationship with a company by offering a budget, you know that year after year you're going to get quality décor rather than leaving it to the winds and hoping that whoever is new enough to want to donate that year will do a good job. Many balloon companies have pet projects that they donate to every year, and are more than happy to give back to those charities. One year, I said yes to every request that came in for donations, and at the end of the year, I found that I had donated more than I had made in revenue- not a good business model. A pet peeve of many balloon artists is the non-profit that calls and says "can you donate and in return we'll give you exposure". I don't want to sound ungrateful, but I get exposure from every event I do, especially the paid ones. Instead, it would be better to ask, "do you offer discounts for non-profits, or here's our budget, what can you do with it?")*

Don't: ask for a proposal for décor and then send it to the next balloon artist for a quote. Steve explains, "When an event planner requests work from a balloon artist, as far as submitting proposals, submitting ideas, or sketches, or photographs, these are proprietary. These are considered our personal work, our personal ideas, and it's considered unethical to share those. Sometimes our uniqueness is what we have to sell, and when you take that uniqueness and give it to someone else hoping to get a cheaper copy. Number one, it won't be the same caliber, and secondly, you've done some damage without knowing it."

Don't: Underestimate the power of a balloon and what can be done with them. – Joette

Don't: Think that you should only spend $100 on the balloons, you could spend thousands of dollars, and have amazing things built. – Joette

Photo and Design by Anne McGovern

Do: Talk to your balloon professional ahead of time, [in the beginning of the planning process] say, "We're doing an event for x number of people, the stage is this big... What do you think you would need to create an amazing event for my client?" – Joette

Do: Allow the balloon professional the opportunity to let you know an estimated budget that can allow them to really give your client that wow they're going for. – Joette *(Note from Sandi: Ask what your balloon pro could do if there were no budget- you just might be surprised at the vision and the price. Even if it's not right for that event, it will give you some ideas on what could be done for future events.)*

Do: Find time to go out to lunch or arrange a meet and greet with your balloon pro to find out what's new in the industry that might make a difference to your events. Find out what the balloon professional can do for you, because you will be amazed at the new things that are out there that don't have to use helium, and that can make an amazing impact on your space. –Joette

Don't: Take it for-granted that the date is booked unless a deposit has been paid, or a contract signed. – Jill

Don't: Make last minute changes, i.e. color changes, balloons need to be ordered in advance and such changes may not be possible. – Jill

Do: Be honest and specific about the actual event time. Your balloon artist will know how far in advance they need to arrive for optimal results. – Jill

Photo and Design by Dianna Glandon

Do: Be specific about the venue and any restrictions that may be faced to enter (i.e. a gated community or security). These delays will have an impact on the amount of time that your balloon artist has to set up and they will need to plan accordingly. – Jill

Don't: Wait until the last minute to call your balloon artist. The sooner you bring them in, the better a partner they can be. – Jill

Don't: Scrimp on the balloon budget. With the proper budget balloons can be transformational. "When budgeting for your event expenses, add an extra $3-$5 to each 'per person' price specifically for balloons to add some color to the space and take it to that next level." – Holland

Don't: Think that balloons by a professional would cost the same as those you could pick up at Party City or do yourself. – Holland

Don't: Assume that balloons are cheap – Dianna

Don't: Assume that balloons are all inflated with helium and can only be put on a string. – Dianna

Do: Have an open mind, and be prepared to answer a lot of questions about your event – Dianna

Do: Expect the unexpected when you're working with a pro because you're going to be very surprised as to how much impact a balloon can have. – Dianna

Do: Call your balloon pro well before your event. Ideally three to four months in advance for major seasonal events. – Dianna *(Note from Sandi: For best results, call balloon person right after securing the venue)*

Do: Familiarize yourself with the ceiling height and rigging points. – Chris

Don't: Try to rig things yourself or hang things off of sprinkler heads or light sockets, those are just big accidents waiting to happen. – Chris

Do: Make sure that your balloon artist has a good reputation, and that they can play well with others. – Chris

Do: Find a company that's excited about getting the job, and is excited about transforming your room. – Chris

Don't: Offer volunteers in lieu of budget, that's never a good idea as they can actually really slow down a project. It's best to leave everything to the professionals. – Chris *(Note from Sandi: if there is a place that you could use your own labor to save money, likely your balloon pro will tell you so.)*

Photo and Design by Holland and Sean Muscio

Do: Order early, give your balloon decorator enough time to prepare and prep for your event and to make sure that everything is ordered and to have plenty of time. – Blenda

Do: Listen to your client and decorator about the color palette; maybe even call enough in advance to get color samples to show the client to make sure they are the right colors. There are probably five shades of pink, for example. – Blenda

Do: Make sure that your balloon decorator has a lot of experience with outdoor décor, because there's definitely a lot of mistakes that can happen. Wind and sun are enemies of balloons, and you have to know how to do it right. It can be done, but you have to make sure that you hire someone who is prepared and has extremely heavy baseplates. – Blenda

Do: Make sure that there is enough time on site for your decorator to actually set up. – Anne

Do: Communicate the client's needs and what the client's vision is to your balloon artist, let them be a partner in the process – Anne

Do: Be clear about strike time and venue restrictions, especially things like no helium or latex rules. – Anne

Do: Make sure that your balloon artist is able to come up with a plan B or C if necessary. – Anne

Photo and Design by Sandi Masori

Photo and Design by Joette Giardina

Photo and Design by Chris Potts

Photo and Design by Sandi Masori

Photo and Design by Blenda Berrier

Favorite Events

I asked my balloon friends to tell me about their favorite and most memorable events or designs. I loved hearing their stories and seeing the photos of their incredible designs.

Tammy: "My favorite design would have to be my kissing frogs from Float, when I won first place there and Designer of the Year. It's my favorite because it had the biggest impact, everyone just fell in love with it."

Photo and Design by Tammy Corzine

Tammy: "My other favorite would be the two palm trees with a hammock and a guy laying in the hammock."

Photo and Design by Tammy Corzine

Tammy: "One of the best events that I did was a corporate Christmas party. We had one that they wanted to do a Vegas themed Christmas party. Their boss was a very traditional 'red and green' type of person, who was apprehensive about even using balloons to start with. The team that he had planning the event decided they wanted to do something fun, a little more outrageous. We actually lined the hallway with black Christmas trees with red ornaments with flashing lights inside of them. We also did over-the-top centerpieces using the tapers and non-rounds with flashing lights in all the centerpieces, and a big balloon wall backdrop. It was all really over the top and looked like it belonged in Vegas. Then for the boss we did a little scene with a fireplace and a Christmas tree, to bring that sense of tradition in for the boss."

Photo and Design by Tammy Corzine

Tammy: "One of the most fun events that I've done was for Proctor and Gamble. They have an annual dinner dance. They pretty much come to us with a budget and a theme and the main areas that they want decorated, and just let us run with it. So it was really fun, on the dance floor we put eight foot tall balloon lava lights with color changing lights inside. We also did big flowers, and a big 'groovy' in sculpted letters; it was about 8' by 12-15' long. Just really cool."

Photo and Design by Tammy Corzine

Tammy, who also has a retail store, mentioned her most popular cash and carry item: "I call them number columns, we take the big foil balloon numbers and turn it into Mickey Mouse or theme it up to whatever theme they want."

Photo and Design by Tammy Corzine

Steve: "The most successful event that we did was the 2012 Halloween and Party Expo. We get sent to Houston every January to do the balloon décor for the Halloween and Party expo, and they wanted to have something really big as far as the sculpture goes. I knew I had some friends there who could help me out, but I wasn't sure what kind of equipment we would have. They wanted a giant cake. I had to design it so that it could be completely free-standing on its own. We couldn't rely on having access to base plates, couldn't rely on rigging it. I wanted to make it completely self-supporting. As the construction was going on, I didn't think it was going to work. And it almost didn't, it was up and down, roller coaster all over the place and finally, in the end, it did. But it literally was like you pop the last balloon into place, and everything went perfectly. It was very nerve racking, but in the end, it worked out beautifully. I was really proud of it. It was almost 30' wide and about 20' high. The only kind of support was that the candles in it had helium. There wasn't a single base plate, pole or rig line in it at all."

Photo and Design by Steve Jones

Joette: "I think one of my most memorable events was a Bat Mitzvah for a young lady who loved to shop. Her mom had spent years getting things for this event. She wanted every single table to look like a different store. It was really rewarding to see all the excitement that this mom and daughter had for the mitzvah, and being able to put all the components together. To take this whole living room full of things and being able to create really fun and funky centerpieces with them, and then adding the balloons to it to give that extra wow and color."

Photo and Design by Joette Giardina

Jill: "My favorite event was one of the Susan G Komen events- it was our largest outdoor event, we spent a day and a half setting it up. We started decorating on Friday afternoon, straight through to Saturday morning, so it was pretty much a campout. We had huge arches, spanning four lanes, created out of helium and 16" balloons. It went up and over. It was really cool looking, especially from an aerial view. This was the first year that we had done mile markers, so we had mile markers all up and down, so everyone knew what mile they had reached, or what K they had hit, so they knew when they were getting close to the finish lines. We also did a start arch- that one was even larger, spanning over five lanes."

Photo and Design by Jill Shortreed

Jill: "Some of my most notable events were Bruce Springsteen's Stone Pony Rising album release, we were contracted to decorate the Asbury Park Boardwalk. We also just recently did a fundraising event for Elizabeth Colbert Bush, and then we do lots of sporting events, like for the Charleston Battery pro soccer team, The Stingrays and multiple concert venues."

Photo and Design by Jill Shortreed

Holland: "For the last four years we've been part of Bert's Big Adventure. He has a syndicated radio show, and takes about 20 local children and their entire families to Disney World. For the kickoff party, they invite all the kids and families in for breakfast. Then they have the kids and the families come on the show and talk about their illnesses and what's wrong and usually do some kind of gift reveal for them, whether it's a sports figure coming in and saying hello, or whatever. It's always kind of fun and we decorate the ballroom for that kickoff breakfast in whatever the theme is. This year was a carnival theme so we had everything in polka dot balloons. We also made some cool clown sculptures at the entry."

Photo and Design by Holland and Sean Muscio

Holland: "One of our most favorite events was to fill a concert venue with Christmas decor. The client worked for a balloon distributor and after giving us our budget basically said, 'Do whatever you want, as long as it looks good.' Our favorite words! We had arches jumping

Photo and Design by Holland and Sean Muscio

from the stage to the balcony level, columns accented with tinsel placed everywhere, reindeer and penguin sculptures hanging from the ceiling... We even put balloons in the bathrooms! "

Holland: "Another favorite was a really great corporate event which was a circus theme. The client came to us and said, 'we want a circus, tell us what you can make- I want some clowns, I want some sculptures...'. They had a good budget, so we were able to create some really interesting balloon art. We did some clown sculptures, a lion jumping through a hoop, and some other fun stuff."

Photo and Design by Holland and Sean Muscio

Dianna: "The most elaborate balloon event we did was for a fraternity. It was their hundred year anniversary, so we did three balloon drops, sixty centerpieces that were all three footers, which we had at different heights, stage décor and entrance arches. It was very elaborate."

Photo and Design by Dianna Glandon

Dianna: "We made a giant roller coaster, it was 258 feet long. It was pretty cool. We made the roller coaster cars, and balloon kids inside each car. We also made a giant Ferris wheel to go with it, that was a good event."

Photo and Design by Dianna Glandon

Dianna: "Sometimes the most simple events are also the most beautiful. One such event was 400 pink and white balloons on the ceiling inside a ring of linking balloons, with lights hanging down from the balloons, it was absolutely gorgeous."

Dianna: "One of the most memorable set-ups was a thirteen foot rainbow trout that we created. It hung from a tree that was thirty feet in the air. My client is a very prominent architect and he and I worked back and forth for almost six months as he was very particular. It was for a wedding rehearsal dinner, and both families were giant trout fishers. Every balloon was double stuffed so that it matched specifically to the color of a real rainbow trout. It hung thirty feet in the air. It probably took us a couple of evenings to build the frame once we got the scale down. The centerpieces were flies that you would use for trout, but we made them all out of balloons. He didn't want them to have feathers on them, so he cut stones and had all different kinds of stuff made for it."

Photo and Design by Dianna Glandon

Chris: "One of our most unique events was a parade, we made big heads out of balloons that looked like Uncle Sam, so we had these big parade heads walking down. That was kind of fun, making giant parade heads."

Photo and Design by Chris Potts

Chris: "The most elaborate event we did was the 80th birthday of a local businessman. He had it up at a huge venue and his budget for décor (not just balloons) was around $200,000! In the beginning, they were real big on it being a black tie affair, so they wanted a lot of fabric and lights and minimal balloons. When we got there to set up what they had ordered, which was his name- 'Happy Birthday Russell'; they just kept adding on and adding on. They said 'oh my god, I love the way the light hits that...' So we started with just a big arch spelling out his name, and ended up doing some columns as well, huge eight foot columns. They just kept adding on, they would come to us and say 'oh my god, Now we need something for this area' – so we kept putting those together.

In the beginning he wasn't a big fan of balloons, but once we got there that changed. Luckily we started early in the morning, we worked right up until the very end, they also added confetti blowers and more. It was the most interesting event, and the largest budget in the end."

Photo and Design by Chris Potts

Blenda: "We had an event where everything just went perfect, it was an event with a planner. Sometime it's hard working with planners because they have these incredible ideas and visions, often they're very hard, not always feasible. This one was 800-1000 balloons that they wanted in a screened in pool area, and they wanted LED lights in them. That was a challenge, because balloons with LED lights in them don't float as well. When everything was said and done though, this whole entire pool canopy was lit with balloons, it was pretty amazing. Those same planners have sold that design several more times too."

Photo and Design by Blenda Berrier

Blenda: "The most memorable event would be when we did a 10,000 balloon release for the Jacksonville Jaguars half time show during their 9-11 tribute. They wanted to do something spectacular, so they hired us to do a giant release. There were several challenges, we were given volunteers to help us bring the balloons out on the field, and that was a bit of a challenge, to trust them to get the balloons out. It worked; we were flexible, we made it work. In a matter of minutes we were lined up and ready to go. It was also a challenge because I had to understand our Florida state statue, what that meant was we had to prove that the balloons were 100% bio-degradable, and that they were all hand tied (no clips or discs). We were able to produce the correct paperwork, and do it in a way that was compliant with the Florida state statute. We also had to be careful with the logistics, because there was a fly-over and sky divers coming down, and we had to make sure that the last sky diver was on the ground before the balloons went up."

Photo and Design by Blenda Berrier

Anne: "My favorite event was a first birthday where we made a carousel in the middle of the dance floor. It was huge and that was my first large sculpture. It was awesome. She also did a lot of floating three foot balloons, tons of columns and we made a clown. It was great. The worst part was that the venue had an event an hour after it was done, so we had to take it down fast. It was upstairs and we were actually going out to the fire escape and throwing the stuff out to the parking lot and popping it in the parking lot because there was no time to take it down properly in the venue."

Photo and Design by Anne McGovern

Anne: "Another favorite event was doing balloons for the people from Cake Boss. They're fun—I've done like five events for them"

Photo and Design by Anne McGovern

Anne: "One of my most memorable events was a grand opening for Stop and Shop. That was a huge challenge because there were 25 foot ceilings and we made pineapples, cupcakes, ice cream cones and strung

Photo and Design by Anne McGovern

garland – it was a huge event and it went so smoothly. It was so much fun, just creating those pieces and seeing them hanging there."

Since we're all telling our stories, let me add mine here as well... My favorite event was actually an ISES event. I had made a giant martini glass- 6', and some columns that looked like rock walls. The theme was "nightclub" and it was full of planners who didn't like balloons that much- didn't think they were appropriate for high-end events. So I was standing just to the left of the sculpture and some of the "rockwalls" and I was introducing myself to everyone as the designer of the balloons there. And they were looking around, over their heads, around the room, and then finally said to me "I don't see any balloons here". I would just point over to my right, not even 3 ' away at the martini glass and watch their jaw drop as they realized that it was in fact balloons that it was made of.

Photo and Design by Sandi Masori

My most unique event- I guess that would be when Southwest airlines opened up their non-stop to Denver flight from San Diego. They hired me and some penguins (yes, real penguins from Sea World), to fly to Denver on the inaugural flight and go up and down the aisle- the penguins waddling and me handing out penguin balloons that I had pre-made. Then once we got to Denver, we hung out in the terminal for a while, doing a meet and greet there, and then repeated the process on the ride home. It was really fun. They also took a bunch of balloon décor, to connect the décor to Colorado, I made columns that looked like mountains with skiers on them. It was really fun, but oh, how people jump if a balloon pops in the airport, lol.

Photo and Design by Sandi Masori

My most memorable event- We did a giant 10' walk through baseball for the San Diego Padres for Tony Gwynn's retirement. We had to construct it so that it could be rolled onto the field within 5 minutes of the game ending, and be very solid for these players to walk through, and hide the next person in line from the cameras so that each player could get their moment and shot. It was absolutely dizzying wheeling it out onto the field- looking up at the sold-out stadium and the sea of people. This was in the beginning of our career, so when we met with them, and they said that they wanted to have something to hide the players from the camera, and what about a giant baseball- well at the time, we had never done anything like that

Design by Sandi Masori
Photo by The San Diego Padres

before. So we said yes, of course, we can do that. Then we went back to the office and said, "ok, now how are we going to do this". We had some really good mentors and had taken some classes in framing, so we just set out to do it. And it was perfect. One of those events where everything goes exactly the way you want.

Other favorite events of mine have been the stages- I really love bringing corporate logos to life and building these giant branded stage walls. Sometimes I see the pictures online as the profile photos from people who may have been speakers on the stage, and I just love it when I see my balloons in the background. I know that it's so important to have the logo just perfect, for the colors to photograph well, there are so many things to take into consideration, and I love that. I love it when the client walks into the room after we've been there all night, and they come in in the morning and are so excited that it's beyond what they had even hoped, and they just can't get over it.

Photo and Design by Sandi Masori

Photo and Design by Sandi Masori

Photo and Design by Sandi Masori

Some More Of Our Favorite Events

Photo and Design by Chris Potts

Photo and Design by Steve Jones

Photo and Design by Jill Shortreed

Photo and Design by Tammy Corzine

Fails and Saves

No business can ever say that everything goes perfectly all the time, and let's face it, often we learn more from the disasters than the successes. Other times you just have to improvise and think on your feet. I asked my friends about their disasters, do-overs, and the times that some clever thinking saved the day.

Once in a while, it's just smarter to say no to the job than to take it. Dianna tells this story about just such a time:

Dianna: "I just refused a job, because they wanted me to float an eight foot balloon over their structure, and they wanted it to go 170 feet in the air. I started checking on some regulations and there were a lot of regulations, one was you have to have a rapid release system so that if the balloon were to get away it could immediately by popped. There was another regulation concerning things floating over 150 feet, so that planes don't fly into it, and several others. I said 'yeah, sorry I'm not doing it.' I feel bad, but I just felt the liability was too big."

I also had a job that I felt had a higher risk factor than I was comfortable with, it was too much liability. It was for a high end birthday party and they wanted a balloon drop over the pool outside in a very large property without anything on which to secure the balloons. So I said we can do it if we put up scaffolding. Outdoors like that, with the kind of torque that you put on the bag to pull the drop, you need a really sturdy rig point. She didn't want scaffolding. Then she suggested using helium filled foil balloons to lift it. Besides still needing solid rig points to anchor it, there's the California balloon laws to consider. When I started to tell her about those laws she told me that she didn't need to know them. They're not the California balloon professional laws, they pertain to everyone who uses balloons in California. I could just see that the pita factor on this was too big, so I politely bowed out. I just had a feeling that no matter what I did the client wouldn't be happy and it would go wrong and end up costing me more than I might make on it. It was actually the first time that I "fired" a client, and though it hurt to do it, I think that I made the right decision.

So, what about those jobs that my balloon friends took, that they look back on and wish that they could either get a do-over, or not take it at all. Let's start with Steve's worst day ever...

Steve: "Big long story   The worst one was February 22, 2002. It was the most awful day ever. We were doing a balloon release for the opening of the Schuster Center in Dayton, Ohio, which was a music hall. And this was a special concert for all the construction teams that built it, so it was a special exclusive concert just for them, and they wanted a 2,000 balloon drop at this venue. We were informed that we would have eight hours on site to inflate the balloons and everything else. That was fantastic, we've got plenty of time. And we were told that because it's a union shop, we would not be allowed to touch any gear, any equipment; we couldn't pull the bags. We couldn't do anything; we would just prep the bags, and they would rig them, and that was it.

"We also had a wedding, literally a mile away from that venue. Another vendor that I did business with, her daughter was getting married; she had hired me to do some balloon décor. So that was the plan, we were just going to take my van, throw everything in the van, drive up. The event was scheduled for Saturday. Friday morning we get a phone call from the client informing us that our eight hour time frame has now turned to 45 minutes.

"So we now have 45 minutes to do this job instead of eight hours. It can't physically be done in that capacity, so we had to rent a truck. At the time, my shop didn't have the capacity to prep that kind of work. Fortunately, one of my clients was a local TV station, and as a favor, they let me use one of their studios to inflate the net. So we had to inflate all the balloons, we had to bag the net, string the net, and then load the net into the truck. And that was a challenge all by itself.

"So then that night, we had extremely cold temperatures, and the window to my van froze, and when I went to roll it down, it broke. So the plan was to take the truck and the van to Dayton. Dayton is not exactly the best crime area. Because I can't roll the windows up, I can't secure the vehicle, so the van can no longer go. So now we're relying totally on the truck. But the truck's having starting issues.

"We have another event on the way there that we drop off, and then we get to Dayton, and we're at the Schuster Center, and we walk in, and of course we brought this net in, and we have 45 minutes to bring the net in, that's it, because we're not allowed to do anything else. So we walk in and the shop steward looks at me and says, 'there you go; have fun.' And I said, 'what are you talking about?' He said, 'what are you talking about? We're at lunch.'

"The 45 minute window that we were given was their lunch break. So this balloon net now had to be rigged and everything else. I said, 'wait a minute, I was told I cannot do this. I was told that it's a union shop, and you guys have to do it.' and he said 'I'm telling you we're going to lunch, and this has to be done by the time we get back.'

"I had to convince someone to give up two minutes of his lunch break to lower the trussing. Then we rigged everything else, and prepared to leave, but now the truck will not start.

"The truck will not start at all. So now we have the venue is upset because we can't get the truck out of the dock. I mean this is a 26 foot truck, or 24 foot truck. We can't get it out of the dock; it's not like you can push it. It was rented, so we called in to have someone come out and service the truck. We were told to call back in two hours to sign up on the waiting list. We weren't even able to get on the waiting list, we had to call back in two hours to get on the list.

"Now the problem is we still have to transport a helium tank and all this other stuff to the other venue, which is a mile away. And, may I add, it's really bad weather; it's snowing; it's ice. I can't push a helium tank for a mile to this venue. So I'm calling my friend, who's the client, but she's the mother of the bride; she's not answering her phone. She's busy doing all this other stuff.

"After an hour and a half we finally got a hold of her. She came flying over, scooped us up, and got us there.

"On top of that, both my partner and I were working with almost dead cell phones, we had no way to recharge them. Just everything was going wrong. So we got to the venue, we did everything in record time, which was great. The church was nice enough to let us store everything there, so we didn't have to worry about retrieving every-thing until Monday.

"But we're still had to get that truck out of there. We dealt with the truck issue for the next six hours, literally trying to get somebody to come get that truck, buy that's a whole other story...

"Now it's time for the drop, and again, I'm not allowed to pull the drop cord, so we have two people that are going to be my pullers. We had one big bag, and we had the line going to the center, so that two people on each end would pull and that would make it faster. I tried to explain to this union guy how to do a balloon drop, and he's like 'I've done this a million times; you don't need to tell me anything. We know what we're doing.'

"And I tried to explain that it's like unraveling a sweater; it's not like a rip cord, but I got serious attitude in response. So we got up there, and I had this flashlight, and I was on the radio headset, and when the cue came up I flashed them both, and they should have done the drop.

"The guy who knew everything was pulling like a rip cord, and it didn't open. It was almost like the infamous Democratic National Convention, the guy was in my ear, 'where are my balloons, pull the balloon.'

"Finally he pulled the cord out and everything went through. We got downstairs, and of course there was the planner standing there. The client was standing there too, and he was looking at me going 'what went wrong?' and the union guy stands right there and said, 'he nev-er told me how to do it.'

"Keep in mind, I was soaking wet because we had to walk back from the church; I was dealing with all the rest of the day, I was exhausted, mentally and physically fried, and I was this close to punching him. It was the icing on the cake for the worst possible day ever.

"Everybody threw me under the bus. The event planner threw me under the bus; the client was angry. The union people threw me un-der the bus. It was one of those days when every time we fixed some-thing, something new came undone.

"I just couldn't wait to get home. By the time we finally got home it was almost two in the morning, because the roads were so bad. When they finally got the truck they towed it away. My dad had a 4-wheel drive, and came and got us. It was quite the evening.

"That was awful. What's funny is when the client was there with the planner was there, it was all an under the bus kind of thing, but in the planner said, 'oh my God I'm so happy you were able to pull it off.' So it was one of those situations where sometimes we end up being under the bus. It's not always the nicest feeling in the world, but if it means long term business, then sometimes you got to roll with it and do what you do. We did do some work for him again, so it wasn't like we were completely written off, but it was awful."

Tammy also had a couple of disasters to share...

Tammy: "We had a big event that we were doing, and it was a lot of onsite stuff that had to be done. The day before when we were prepping I had three of my crew just not show up or call in. The day of setup I had two more people not show up or call in, and even for doing the strike, I had people that didn't show up. My crew just really let me down for that event and we weren't able to get everything done that we were supposed to get done for the client. The event looked amazing, it still looked really great, but there were elements missing that the client wanted, that we just weren't able to complete. That was my biggest disaster. Of course I apologized profusely and offered them a big discount both on that event and on a future one. So we were able to keep the client, and they did use us again, but that was bad."

Tammy: "Another disaster was one of the first big outdoor events I did, before I had any formal training. I didn't know about under-inflating and using bigger balloons and expansion and all of that. We did a corporate event outside for a hospital and we set up this really cool arch with '100' letter balloons on it for their 100th anniversary. Before we left half of the arch was gone because the balloons were popping. It was just a total disaster. Everything that we did under the tent was fine, but this arch was the focal point. Now I know not to let them use dark colors, and I would have used 16" balloons instead of 11" and underinflated them so that they had lots of room to expand with the heat."

Steve also had another disaster to share...

Steve: "In the earlier days of everything there's always jobs that just make you go ugh. The one thought that pops into my head every time is the very first balloon drop I ever did. It was 1,200 balloons; it was three bags. It was on a very low ceiling to begin with, and I was very new to all of this.   I was following the instructions in the kit and everything, so I stitched the bag lengthwise, and then I went back up the edge. But my concern was because the ceiling was so low that the rig line would be in people's way. So I made the horrible mistake of rigging the line back up to the ceiling to come back down again. When you do a balloon drop you want as straight a line as possible. When you start to pull the cord it wants to straighten the line out, it doesn't follow the pattern you want it to follow.

"So here we were standing in this room in front of all these people, pulling the balloon drop, and all it's doing is just lifting the bag up in the air as it tries to straighten that line out.   And eventually, in all three cases, what happened was the bags burst open due to the pressure, so it wasn't really a balloon drop as much as it was a balloon dump. My hands were bleeding afterwards, I didn't know to have gloves, and I had cut my hands open. It was the longest 47 seconds of my life. To make matters worse we had videotaped it, because we wanted to document the effect. So, you can just imagine how well that went over.

"I will say though, as badly as that went, the follow up was good, because we walked in and I took full responsibility for what happened right away.   This was an event planner situation, so you had the client and the event planner standing there. I looked right at the client and took full responsibility, how it wasn't the event planner's fault at all, this was my mistake, please don't punish her. I told her 'We're comping this right now.'

"That's the one gig that always sits in my head, as the 'if I could go back and do again.' The one thing I would have done differently is I might have tried to actually talk them out of the balloon drop, because again that ceiling was so low. It was probably a 10 foot ceiling. But also, I would have made smaller bags, thinner bags, whatever. I would have had enough common sense to say, 'look this may not create the effect you really want to create.' As a newbie that's when I think we're the most dangerous. "

Dianna had a story about the event that she would do- over...

Dianna: "If I had a do-over, it would be a bar mitzvah that we did a little bit over a year ago. The client, asked for all abstract stuff. The balloons went fine, but he also asked us to hang some photos that he had made especially for the event. We hung them and we had a ton of problems with them because the photos kept sliding down. Anyway, when we left, everything looked great. We didn't leave until five or ten minutes after the event started, and then the client called and said everything was crooked and he didn't like it. Then he refused to pay me, so I regret that it didn't look as good as he would have like it to, but if I had to do it over again I would say, 'No I'm not hanging your photos.'"

It wouldn't be fair of me to ask my friends to share their embarrassing stories without sharing some of my own, so here's the event that sticks out in my mind as the worst one ever...

It was a Black Friday event at a mall- 3 stores were having an anniversary celebration, and wanted pretty elaborate décor. They were all in the same outdoor mall. This was pretty early on, but I asked about wind in the area, and of course was told that there never was any. When we did the site inspection, there wasn't anything to worry about. So we went to build it, and this was a serious all night build.

We'd already been working for the past few days on the pieces. There were to be three pieces-- for one of the stores, a giant walk-through juke box with the store logo on it- it was about 10' x 15' - huge, the other store had two marble columns with a golden vase at the top, and a marble arch connecting them. The bottoms and tops of the columns were square, made using a distortion technique that wraps pieces of foamboard into deflated balloons- (so you can get the texture and color), but use it in a 2-d way, and the centers were made from the same balloons, with the marble texture. They came out perfect. The puzzle technique is so much work, but you can get such great results with it. Anyway, the last one was the giant Old Navy sign with the people and the kids.

In San Diego we have a weather condition called a Santa Ana, it's really fast hot wind- causes all sorts of issues. So we were there at 9pm setting up and we had to be done by 5 am. We started with the columns because they were the simplest. Then we moved across the plaza to the other store to make the big juke box. As we were making balloons there was a lot of static in the air, and balloons were popping everywhere- we were using a pearl dark blue for the jukebox. We had underinflated it, but there was a lot of static and they were popping like crazy. We were fighting the popping balloons, and replacing them left and right. We had to improvise colors as we ran out of our extras with all the popping. Finally we got it finished and it looked good. After all that it looked really good. And luckily, right then the client came up and saw it, but we never got pictures of it. It was before all the phones had cameras and we never got the picture.

Anyway as the client was talking to us, it started to get windy, and the décor started shaking. We had built it all really stable, for normal conditions, we weren't expecting the Santa Ana to come through and turn into a wind tunnel. Because of how the buildings faced each other it really magnified the wind. We tried to tuck the columns in under the overhang a little, and cut the arch so it wouldn't act as a sail. My husband and one of our employees were on either side of the jukebox, just trying to hold it down, and the wind came through and broke it in half- just tossed my husband to one side and our employee to the other.

The square parts of the column were ripped off because of the wind, and one of the poles was bent- they were really strong winds. We still hadn't set up Old Navy yet, so we had to leave it there and just try to salvage what we could and take the rest out to the truck. We had to go and put up Old Navy, which was on the other side of the mall, in a more open area. We got Old Navy up, and by this time had gotten someone from the mall to help us rig it to the roof with chains, so that one stayed up and we got the pictures. Even though we managed to save that one, I left that day thinking 'this is it, I'm done in this business, I'm just quitting.' It was awful. The only saving grace was that the client had actually seen it before everything went wrong. From then on I'm very careful about explaining the potential issues with outdoor décor and assume the worst conditions for wind and sun.

Photo and Design by Sandi Masori

Jill also had a story to contribute...

Jill: "My do- over was a Komen event. We were planning on doing logo walls for them. Their theme was superheroes and we were going to use a grid system. We did not open up the packages ahead of time, and when we got there we found we had faulty panels, so we had to improvise. If I could go back and do it again, I would have checked my product when it came in, instead of just loading it and going. But, we had used the product many times before and never had a problem, but this one time we did. After a lot of frustration and everybody getting short and tired because it was 3 am, we just decided that was it, time to go home. So we came up with an alternative plan. I felt really bad, but the alternative décor looked great, it just wasn't what we had promised them, so that would be my do over."

Anne also learned a lesson from her disaster...

Anne: "I had one event, and it was for a major corporation, and we had to make a giant 6' heart that was being hung up. They didn't want us hanging it, so we left it for them to do. Well, I get a phone call after we leave the event saying the frame fell apart. The event was actually the next day, so I said to her, 'I could go back and fix it, but I think that I'll make something else instead.' So I ended up making a puffed heart instead. I just worried that going back and trying to fix it wouldn't work out- I just didn't know whether they did something to it or what, and when we got back there I saw that somebody had taken it and bent it, so thank G-d we did what we did. From then on, I hang my own stuff if at all possible, or I don't leave until it's actually up."

Chris had this to add...

Chris: "Well, I'll tell you there's really one disaster that just keeps kind of going through my mind. The gig was a balloon drop for a man who was running for governor of New York. We made six bags, each with 1,000 balloons that would drop after he announced his candidacy. The people who hired us wanted to save a little bit of money, so they wanted the volunteers to pull the strings on these six drops, and just have me there supervise.

"So I said, 'okay.' I had everything set up. I told them to pull the strings, and we coordinated the times. Well, when it came time to pull the strings, everything went fine, except one girl had her string, and she just didn't pull it hard enough. She got nervous that it wasn't going to pull, and she let go of the pull string. It was still tied on, so that wasn't the issue, but she went figured it was a good idea to untie the rope that I had tied from the bag to a fixture that was holding the bag to the ceiling.

"So she untied these knots, it took her like two, three minutes, and I'm standing on the other side of the balcony about 50 feet away, just watching this, saying 'oh my god, this is not going to end well if she unties that knot.' Sure enough, she untied it, and then the rope flew away, and the bag started coming down with the balloons in it over the crowd, and luckily there was just a little knot or something in the rope, and it got hung up on a bolt in the ceiling.

"Five bags dropped, and one bag was kind of hanging at an angle. If that would have fell, if the line would have come through, the net would have fallen right on the crowd, so I was just holding my breath for the last 20 minutes when he was giving his speeches, hoping that the net would not fall into the crowd.

"That experience reinforces my, 'it's -nice -to -save −money- but -let −me- just- have −my- people- do- it- so- there's -no −surprises' policy. When you do events, and any time you rig anything above people's heads, you have to always think of what's the worst case scenario? And that's one of the great thing about balloons, we suspend things, and if it would fall for some reason, it usually wouldn't be a big issue, because it's just balloons. Even if it's a big balloon, it's still not going to do any damage. But still, that's one event that I still think about."

Photo and Design by Chris Potts

Sometimes some quick thinking and a bit of improvisation by a seasoned professional can make all the difference. Here are some of those stories:

Dianna: "We were hanging some balloons at an event center and the magpole, (a long pole made for placing magnets on the ceiling), always stays in the van, but somehow it wasn't there. We had to hang it, and to go across town and come back would have been an hour and we didn't have time to do it, so we thought 'what if we take some magnets and attach them to this other pole' that we had in the car. So we took the magnets and taped them to the end of a pole, and by golly we had a magpole and we were able to hang everything."

Photo and Design by Dianna Glandon

Steve: "A couple of years ago where we did a Christmas party for the USS Stennis, which is a big Navy ship. And that was just massive sculpture stuff everywhere, and just a lot of work, again three or four days of just constant inflation and blowing up everything. But that was an interesting problem, because the client was actually someone who served on the ship.

"We did all the work through the planner, and she's the one that we pitched the idea to. She'd approved it and everything else. Well, she had no idea what the end client had done in the past, and when I walked in with all these incredible sculptures and everything else, he was like, 'so where's everything else?' They were used to having an absolute explosion of helium balloons and foils, and stuff everywhere.

"I wasn't privy to this; I had no idea what they had done before, so actually he was upset with me almost the whole time, because I wasn't doing what he wanted. And I politely explained to him that why I did it. It ended up okay, and at the end he was very happy. It worked out. It could have been nicer, but it worked out well."

Photo and Design by Steve Jones

Jill: "South Carolina is not a cool weather state, so we have to deal with a lot of heat. The sun is really blaring, and we have high humidity. There's only so much we can do to protect the balloons from popping, but we do everything we possibly can, whether it be pre-stretching balloons, and downsizing them. Our outside décor is more expensive than our inside décor, and that's because of the extra labor that goes into trying to ensure that it's the best quality that we can give you for an outdoor event. We do a lot of outside décor, and it's challenging, but we do it. We've done soccer players that have gone outside the Charleston Battery in sculpture format. Those were a little more difficult because of the sizing, but we did it. We do a lot of our event poles, and a lot of pom-poms. We have even installed them on our interstate, because our soccer team backs up to the interstate where their billboard is. That's really rough, because of the wind, the traffic, and the pollution that goes past that. Our clients know that we really take the time to make sure that everything we do is installed correctly and safely, and it's not going to come off and hurt or hit somebody with a pole. We use some pretty substantial weights, and poles, and rods, and anchoring systems."

Photo and Design by Jill Shortreed

Tammy: "We do a lot of improvising. A 260 can fix just about anything. There are lots of times where there's something that's missing from the toolbox and we have to get kind of creative."

Holland: "You have to improvise almost every day. They're balloons, they pop, so you either fix it, or, let's say someone else packed the vehicle, and didn't include the extra balloons. So you have to figure out how to fix the pop. If something needs to be a little bit taller, you find a way to make it taller. There's always improvising. Sometimes you get to the space, and the wall you built isn't quite big enough, or the columns need to be a little bit taller, because even though you quoted the customer a certain thing, if it doesn't look right. I want it to look right, so I'm going to make it look right, because my name's on this, we want it to be perfect, so we're going to make sure it looks good before we leave."

Jill: "Sometimes the client will tell us the wrong ceiling height on something that was supposed to be installed on the ceiling. That happened with one of our proms, we were told the ceiling heights, by the venue manager, and she gave us the wrong height. We were not able to reach the ceilings to do the installation that we were supposed to do, so we just had to change around the décor for the prom. It wasn't that big of a deal, the prom committee was tickled pink. They've used us over and over again, but we have since purchased a laser tape, so we can go in and measure for ourselves, so we don't have to trust what someone says because sometimes that information's incorrect."

Joette: "We did two proms on the same day in Orlando and it was on the Disney property, so we thought there would be no problem going from point A to point B. We'd do one and then the other. The first one went without a hitch. But the second one, well, we were sitting there and the electricity went off in the entire ballroom and hallway where we were trying work. There were a couple of plugs in the lobby that we could reach with extension cords, so we got a couple of lamps from the lobby so we could work in the dark, so that was kind of interesting. It was the last place I thought I would ever have to bring my own power supply... that's why being early and having a large team is good."

Photo and Design by Tammy Corzine

Of course I also have such stories. Here's one of my favorite ones. We were supposed to set up décor for a breakfast, so it was an o dark thirty load-in. The security guard was supposed to let us into the room, which was in its own building. We got there at 3am like we were supposed to and went to the front desk, and the front desk guy didn't know what we were talking about. He tried to call the security guard, but he never answered. We waited for about 30 min or so and then said we have to get started. We went back to the event room and still no security guard and it's still locked. We wait a bit more and it was a little windy, just enough that I didn't want to inflate the balloons outside in the open, then luckily we realized that there was a bathroom across the way- like just across the path. So we went into the bathroom and started blowing up balloons there- we started with the helium first since we needed electricity for the air work, and we just did everything we could until someone finally came and then we worked as fast as we could. It worked out in the end, but it was close.

Blenda summed it up pretty well...

Blenda: "Sometimes you just have to make it work, and that's kind of what we do, that's why people hire us, because we're going to make it happen. If they've ordered a ten foot column and there's a nine foot ceiling, and we have to make it work, we're going to pull out a saw to fix that column."

Photo and Design by Blenda Berrier

In most of these stories, the client probably never knew the difference, or if they did, the guests certainly didn't. That's one of the benefits of using a professional balloon company, we always have a "plan B" in our back pocket, or at least the knowledge and experience to come up with one at a moment's notice.

Photo and Design by Anne McGovern

Photo and Design by Chris Potts

Milestones

Design by Sandi Masori
Photo by Gary Schacker

Design by Sandi Masori

Photo and Design by Sandi Masori

Design by Sandi Masori

Birthdays

As a balloon artist, no matter what you specialize in, or where you target your marketing, you're going to get asked to do birthday parties. Some of those birthday parties are pretty standard, and some of them are crazy over the top. I have to admit, both as a mom, and as a balloon artist, I'm personally in favor of the crazy over the top ones. It's not just kids parties though, some of the best birthday parties are the ones for the adults. I always like to say that balloons are perfect for both the young in age and the young at heart.

Since birthdays are such a popular time to use balloons, I asked my balloon friends what the best parties they had done were, and what trends they see.

Tammy: "50 is our most popular age for adult parties. We did a scuba diver that was actually for a 50 year old birthday party. Most of the adult ones don't have a theme though, they just pick and go with that. We get some of the higher ages too; we've done quite a few 80th birthday parties for example. They really want to do something to signify that 80th birthday. So we'll do a lighted balloon with '80' on it in vinyl to customize it for them. As for trends, they tend to go more for the creative stuff. 50 to 80 I would say are our most popular ages , and they just want something that's fun and bright and cheerful. We don't get a lot that want the 'over the hill' and the black and the dark, dreary things.

"We also do a fair amount with the megaloons, the big numbers, to bring the age into it. Most of the birthdays that we've done like to theme it around something that the birthday person, loves or does. For example, we did the scuba diver party, because the guy was a scuba diver, so we made a scuba diver sculpture, some palm trees, and a guy laying on a hammock.

"It was a fairly extravagant party; we don't usually get that extravagant with most of the birthday parties. They don't have the budget for that. They'll pick something like rock star, because the kid's into music. For the kids' parties, they are starting to theme them the same way they do for Mitzvahs."

Photo and Design by Tammy Corzine

Holland: "We try and work around the number, if it's a milestone birthday, whether it's making a sculpture of the letter or using the number balloons that are out there, and then adding to them. Sometimes we put them on a column, or with ribbon streamers, or we may add balloon curls. We've done a pirate party, for example, with spiders and swords, and the skull and crossbones.

"We try to take the theme and take it to the next level for the customer. I have plenty of clients who just want classic balloons on ribbons, but we do get clients who will allow us to take to that next place and help them do something a little different.

"We do adult parties too; it can be fun, for example, we did a 40th birthday party, and they were using flowers, and daisies. So we made some giant balloon daisies that were around the space as you came into the party, and by the bar. Everybody really enjoyed those.

Photo and Design by Holland and Sean Muscio

Instead of it being a sad, 'look who's 40' party, black and white, 'over the hill' kind of thing, it was a fun, springy kind of party. We've also done the 'look who's 40' parties too, where we've taken black and white balloons, used balloon curls, and added in silly writings on pieces of paper, mounted them in columns, and whatever else we decorated. We work with the customer to help them come up with a theme."

Photo and Design by Holland and Sean Muscio

I asked Holland what areas she sees needing décor the most. Here's what she had to say

Holland: "We find the two biggest areas are your entrance and your stage. Sometimes the stage is not as big of a deal, so they may not do anything there, but they want to really wow people when they walk in the door. That's always nice, it helps to get people excited for the event they're going into."

And on the topic of challenges, and things that would be useful for planners to know, Holland had this to say:

Holland: "To me it helps to know where your venue is, and to be familiar with the venue. Then you work with the client to find out what their goals are, because I hate it when someone calls me and says, 'I just want to get five dozen balloons delivered.' And you're like, 'yeah, but what are you going to do with them?' Often, by the time you're

Photo and Design by Steve Jones

done, for that same amount of money, you've turned it into something else that's going to look better than five or ten dozen balloons.

"I feel that it is important to try to find out what the client's end goal is. Do we want to have something interesting to welcome them in? If so, let's do some football player sculptures at the beginning for example. We try to express to the customer all the varieties of opportunities, things that we can create for them. We've got sculptures, we can do balloons on ribbon, we can do arches; there's all different kinds of things to help fill that space, to help them reach their goal in their budget, and to help create exactly the feel for the event that they're looking for."

Photo and Design by Tammy Corzine

Communions

Being Jewish, I have to admit that I don't know much about the Christian life cycle events. One of my balloon friends, Anne, does a lot of communions, so I welcomed the opportunity to learn about them, and their particular needs. Here's what Anne had to share...

Anne: "Christenings happen all the time. They're all year long. You're supposed to have it within a certain time after the baby's born, but I think those rules kind of went out the window years ago. They're a lot of fun. I'm finding a big trend is going away from the religious aspect of it. They'll do something more for an impact piece or something like that.

"Communions happen during such a short period of time. There's say 110 kids in each communion, and everybody does their communion together. I think the most we ever decorated was 17 in one day. It is crazy. We put limits on it now, and set up a lot of them the day before. Some churches will even have two communions; they'll have a 10:00am and a 1:00pm. So as soon as they know their date, everybody's booking their party. For example, I already have six communions booked for this coming May *(Sandi's note- this interview took place over the summer)*.

"One church could have 200, 300 kids on one day. They have to go scramble for the halls, and then they call us, so that's good. We limit what we do, and we won't do some stuff because it wouldn't last. We'll only do things that will last longer so that we can do them ahead of time. It is such a short period of time, approximately from the end of April to the very beginning of June. You've got six weeks and that's it. The parties generally are off site in different halls, or hotels, or venues.

"There's been a trend where it's gotten bigger. In the last two years it's become more like bar and bat mitzvahs where we're doing dance floors, and floating topiaries and much more elaborate centerpieces, and really nice things.

"We're doing a lot of the full size crosses with their names, floating angels, and there's definitely much more custom work than what it was. It used to be 'we want three balloons on a weight.' This past season was our best communion season ever. I enjoyed it because we were doing such nice stuff for people. I enjoy adding the tulle and the feathers. We definitely do more girl communions than boy ones though."

Photo and Design by Anne McGovern

Anne continued, "They always want centerpieces. This year was the first time we did some dance floors; I never had the dance floors before for a communion, so that was a lot of fun. Centerpieces, name card table and the gift table are more traditional. Usually they also want something next to the DJ, but this was the first year that I had much more upscale communions.

Photo and Design by Anne McGovern

Photo and Design by Tammy Corzine

Photo and Design by Sandi Masori

Photo and Design by Anne McGovern

Bar Mitzvahs

Whereas I don't feel as though I know a lot about the Christian life cycle events, I can honestly say that I know a lot about Bar Mitzvahs. The Bar/ Bat Mitzvah is a coming of age ceremony for Jewish children. In reform and conservative traditions it happens at the age of 13 for boys and girls alike. For Orthodox children, girls will become a Bat Mitzvah at 12 years old, and boys will become a Bar Mitzvah at 13. The kids spend years preparing for their Bar Mitzvah, learning to

Photo and Design by Sandi Masori

chant a Torah portion and all of the accompanying prayers in Hebrew. They also will deliver a speech on how they interpret their portion and what it means to them. It's much more than just the party, though of course that's what we in the event industry most often see. At the time of this writing, my own son is preparing for his Bar Mitzvah, and as a Bar Mitzvah mom, I can tell you that it takes a lot of commitment on the part of the whole family.

I have to say, I like being on the vendor side of the Mitzvahs much more than on the parent side of it. There are so many things that you're dealing with as a Bar Mitzvah mom, things that have nothing to do with the party at all. So as a parent, to have someone to help you with those other things, all the details of the party, it's a great relief. To know that you're working with professionals, and that you don't have to babysit them, or worry about whether or not they'll deliver, makes such a difference.

Even though I have decorated a lot of Mitzvahs, I wanted to get some other perspectives on the needs of this event. Every balloon artist I know, if they live in an area that has a Jewish population, will decorate a Bar Mitzvah at some point. Bar Mitzvahs, maybe even more than any other event, lend themselves to balloons. It's the biggest event in a Jewish child's life, and the party should be all about them.

Although every one of the balloon artists I interviewed does Bar Mitzvahs, I especially asked Anne and Joette to share their thoughts with me. Here's what they had to say...

Anne: "The children are usually involved, sometimes they have a theme, sometimes they just have a color scheme, and sometimes they have no idea what they want. But they're 13, and they're so much fun, because usually they want something fun.

"I'm very careful, because I try not to talk or show anything to the child that might be out of the parents' price range. I try to have the conversation with the parents beforehand, getting an idea of what their budget is, what they want to spend. I'm a mother of three, so I wouldn't want anybody suggesting things to my kids that were out of my price range; you know how kids are so impressionable, 'yeah I want my name sculpted with lights,' for example. There may be other options that are less expensive than the full sculpture of their name. So I try to work with them on that.

"The other thing is that every temple has their rules; they're all different. I'm not Jewish, but I know that it doesn't matter whether you're conservative, orthodox, whatever, every temple seems to have their own rules. If the reception will be at the temple, I make sure I find out what their rules are and try to be respectful.

"Some of the temples, you have to go in Friday afternoon to set up for Saturday, some you have to be out by 1:00, some by 6:00; so it all depends on the temple. You have to be very careful, that you're not disrespectful. I think this is key.

"I find that probably 80% of the kids know what they want. They go to a lot of bar and bat mitzvahs, all their friends are having their bar and bat mitzvahs in the same year. So they know what they want, or what they don't want. They don't want something that the last kid just had.

Design by Sandi Masori
Photo by Alan Krause

"Some typical balloon creations that we do for the Bar Mitzvahs are ... well, the kids love their name. We probably do the foil, megaloon name arches every weekend. *(Note from Sandi: the foil balloon arches have to be against the wall in California due to the California Balloon Laws which state that every foil balloon has to be individually anchored).*

"They love their name. Three foot balloons are also huge, as is anything that is going to match their theme, whether it's a candy theme, or Hollywood, or sports. For the boys it's a lot of sports. If the child doesn't have any theme, then we just to make it fun, different, and unique so that it's going to represent them.

"I recently just added the bathroom basket because every bar and bat mitzvah has a bathroom basket, and the moms are stressed out, and they have a lot of work as it is. So she's like 'can you do it for me?' And I'm like, 'sure.' So I just added that on. The sign in boards usually go with their theme. Candle boards are also popular.

"I think the entrance is very important. Table centerpieces are also very important. Then would be your dance floor. Your head table is

Photo and Design by Anne McGovern

also very important. Everything depends on the budget, and the room. If you have a beautiful room you might not have to do as much, but I try to tell people that if they do something at the entrance, especially if they don't have a very large budget, then we can try to do something that's moveable, that way later they can bring it in and put it next to the DJ. We definitely try to encourage them to do something at the entrance that creates the atmosphere that they're entering the party now; that says 'we're going to go have fun.'

"Probably the biggest challenge, is the time to set up. If a venue has back to back events, for example when they're clearing one out at 5:30, and the next one's starting at 7:00. And they'll tell you, 'okay you have 45 minutes to set up.' That's a huge challenge. Certain venues don't work very well with you, and you have other ones who just bend over backwards, so it depends on the venue.

"That's another thing you learn, you definitely learn to be in contact with your venue early to see what time you can set up, and make sure they know what you're doing. If you don't have a lot of time you need to have enough staff, and you need to have a truck, and have everything ready to go. So that is always a huge challenge, but it's always workable; you do it, and if it's not workable than you just got to find a way to do it in the parking lot, whatever you have to do, you do it.

"As I mentioned, it's really important to know the rules of the synagogue, because if you have to set up the day before, you have to make sure that it is something that's going to last, whether you hi-float it, or we do a lot of air filled décor. We do a lot of lomey poles, and air filled centerpieces, and columns-- items that are going to last, and designs that are going to last even if the air is not ideal in the venue over night.

"I usually will sit and down and will talk with the client, and say, 'this is what your options are.' I think they appreciate that; I'm not going to sell them anything that's not going to last, or that's not going to work the next day.

"I've run into issues with Kosher, I actually brought in a cup of coffee one time I wasn't allowed to. So I wouldn't do that again. Some of the venues that we go to have a kosher kitchen. They allow, kosher caterers to come into their kitchen, and they're usually ones that let me in, because they're there early."

Photo and Design by Anne McGovern

Joette shared her favorite Bat Mitzvah set up with me.

Joette: The shopping mitzvah. We made a bat mitzvah girl reading the Torah for the candy table, and she stood about six and half feet tall. Then every centerpiece was about four feet tall, plus the helium balloons above it, which went another 15'. The ceilings there were about 20 feet tall, and we pretty much filled that space, and had shopping bags and goodies just flowing out of them. We had to have two eight foot tables for the candy table. The jawbreakers were in a huge punch bowl, and over the dance floor there was what we called a 'reverse pillow canopy'.

"Using link o loon balloons, we created this whole canopy that typically would be something that people would use a backdrop for a wall. We hung it from the four corners, so it draped over the top of the dance floor; it kind of looked like a princess pillow. Then we wrote out the bat mitzvah girl's name, 'Sarah', out of five foot tall balloon sculptures, and just had balloons everywhere.

"So it was balloons everywhere you looked, plus all the cool stuff for the shopping, the stores, and the signs. It made for a really fun night. You could see the lighting from the DJ bounce off of the canopy over the dance floor, and then the confetti was shot out over the dance floor too, so just a really fun, awesome evening."

Photo and Design by Joette Giardina

I agree, sounds like lots of fun. J In my opinion, the most important area of the Bar/ Bat Mitzvah to decorate is the dance floor. This is really where everything should be happening. When I have clients working with a tight budget, I recommend that they decorate the dance floor. Even if there is nothing special on the tables, but you have a fun dance floor treatment, it will set the ambiance and invite people to get up and celebrate. Balloons are a great option for Bar Mitzvahs because it should be a whimsical celebration. I'm amazed at the clients I've had who wanted to decorate in all flowers, or other fragile elements. You don't say anything to them, but you're thinking, 'where is the kid in this? I know that this décor isn't for him, what's representing him?'

Photo and Design by Sandi Masori

Lately there has been a trend to go back to basics. A popular idea is a Mitzvah Basket Centerpiece base.... The base of centerpiece is a basket put together by Mitzvah kid which will be donated somewhere after the party. Balloons are added to the top. This is a good idea to mention to the client, because often Bar Mitzvah moms are looking for a way to connect the party back to something more meaningful. A word of caution though, be sure to put a note or sign clearly stating the purpose of the basket so that it doesn't get accidentally acquired by a guest.

I have seen many blunders made on the part of both planners and balloon people alike, so I want to share a little more about the culture and some of the things that are useful to know when working with a Bar/ Bat Mitzvah parent.

One of the things that's important to know about Bar Mitzvahs is the difference in the types of Judaism and what that might mean to setting up the reception. There are three main levels of Judaism, Reform, Conservative and Orthodox. Reform tends to focus more on the cultural identity of being Jewish, and not necessarily on the rules as much. While it's unusual to see food that is specifically unkosher, often the food might be "kosher style," this means that although there is no hechsher on the food, they're still not serving pork, shellfish, or mixing milk and meat. If the reception is in a reform synagogue, it's probably ok to go in on Saturday to set it up. Orthodox is the opposite, they keep every law to the letter, and often have fences built around those laws as well. If the reception is in the synagogue, it will need to be set up on Friday and left for the Sat party. The food will be strictly kosher, and be very careful of anything that you bring in.

One of the biggest places I see mistakes being made is with candy bouquets and candy buffets. If you are doing a Bar/ Bat Mitzvah for an Orthodox family, make sure to check the hechshers (kosher symbols on food packages). The third "level" is Conservative, which could lean more towards reform or orthodox. In general they tend to keep more of the rules, like not mixing milk and meat, or not eating shellfish, but may not need the right hechsher on every item. As a general rule, I'd advise being more aware of it than your client- they will appreciate your knowledge and sensitivity even if they don't keep that level of Kosher.

Generally speaking, the "OU" hechsher is the most common and reliable one. I would advise though, no matter what level of Judaism they practice, if it's not specifically kosher, don't bring it into the venue. That way you won't accidentally make a mistake. Below is a list of some of the many hechsher symbols.

Please note that these are just some examples
There are many more Kosher symbols, and not all of them
have equal standing. If you aren't sure, check with the office of the
synagogue you will be working with.

For decorating purposes, check hechsher of candy to be put on tables. Also make sure that if you're planning to scatter Hershey's kisses on table, check to see if they're serving meat. Check their level of observance, and ask them if they care about having dairy chocolate w/ a meat meal... Even if they don't care about keeping kosher, they will appreciate you knowing enough to ask.

When planning a Bar/ Bat Mitzvah, find out where the reception will be held and if it's at the synagogue, check on the rules for setting up on Saturday. Sometimes the client is not aware of the rules, so it's always a good idea to check with the synagogue itself. Many Bar Mitzvahs are held in the social hall of the synagogue. Some synagogues will let you come in and build on Shabbat. Some synagogues will let you come in on Shabbat only if you're NOT Jewish. Some synagogues will only let you come in on Friday.

Other things that are useful to know;

Orthodox men/ women don't touch. A good rule of thumb, don't offer your hand to a member of the opposite sex, unless they offer first... If you're not sure what their level of observance is, there are signs you can look for. Some signs you're working with someone ultra-orthodox: Man has a beard, payis (special sideburns), and a kippa (or black hat). The Woman likely is wearing a wig, hat or scarf covering her hair, a skirt going past her knees and a shirt going past her elbows.

Another place that I see a lot of mistakes being made is in the terminology. The people are Jewish, the religion is Judaism, Hebrews are an ancient people and Hebrew is a language. When someone calls you to talk to you about a "Simcha" (a happy life event), the best response is "Mazal Tov" (congratulations). Other "Simchas" that have big parties are the Bris (ritual circumcism for a baby boy), the "Upshoren" (ritual first hair cut for a 3-year old boy), and of course weddings.

If you are asked to plan an Orthodox, or Ultra-Orthodox event, they may have two dance floors, one for men and one for women. Likely they will want a "Mehitza" between the two, so that the men won't see the women dancing. You will not find this at reform or conservative events, but you will find it at many Orthodox events.

Photo and Design by Sandi Masori

Photo and Design by Sandi Masori

Sweet 16s and Quinceaneras

Photo and Design by Sandi Masori

Sweet 16s and Quinceaneras are pretty similar. A quinceanera is the Hispanic coming of age for a 15 year old girl. A sweet 16 is the coming of age for 16 year old girls of many different cultures.

Joette finds herself doing a lot of Sweet 16s and had this to share with us...

Joette: "For sweet 16s sometimes people just enjoy having anything that has the number 16, that could be a huge eight foot sculpture, or five foot sculpture, or the foil balloons that are sparkly and shiny. A lot of times you're using the silver accent or a gold accent with those, and making sure the 16 is prevalent everywhere.

Photo and Design by Joette Giardina

"The other thing is I've seen with a lot of my sweet 16s is they want to have that personalization, so on their centerpieces they'll often have photos of the child. We put them into an air filled centerpiece, with really creative props.

"One of my favorites was a sweet 16 where she was very nostalgic, and she and her best friend had gone and taken their pictures at a vintage clothing store. They tried on different clothes, took the pictures, and then they had black and white photos made. We put those inside their centerpieces with small little balloons and twisty balloons, and it was very elegant with accents of lighting and pearls and old time records. We made it a very vintage look, and very personalized to them, but it still had the balloons and was very fun.

Photo and Design by Joette Giardina

"For sweet 16s they seem to really like to have a cool centerpiece for each table, and then to have something really cool at their cake table, or cupcake table as it may be. Typically that would be a taller centerpiece that's at least 32 inches tall. Then maybe they'll have some really cool clusters of helium balloons coming out the top, or even an air filled sculpture that's five or six feet tall. The other area they typically like to have is a photo area. So we'll drop a backdrop of fabric, and then put either a balloon wall or balloon columns in their theme, so that they have a really nice place to take their photos throughout the evening.

"Typically all of them have a dance floor, so that's another area that they really enjoy decorating. Neon has been very popular lately. We take neon lighting and wrap the poles in balloons with the neon lights, and incorporate that with the helium balloons and air filled balloons just to give a really cool 'wow' effect. As the lights go down the balloons really stand out for the dance floor, because that's where the kids spent most of their evening.

"The number one challenge for either event is to really know your ceiling heights, know where the air conditioning system intakes and outtakes are, so that you know how your décor is going to be affected by those issues, and then also just knowing the limitations of the space. There are some venues that do not allow helium balloons due to having had issues in the past with ceiling fans, or that have super high ceilings where they don't know how they would ever get a balloon down if it got lost.

"A lot of times event planners don't even know that there are options in balloons that are non-helium, so if they walk into a space the event planner may be told 'no balloons are allowed,' but really it's no helium balloons are allowed. The really cool creations that we can create out of air filled designs on framework will be perfectly fine in that venue.

Photo and Design by Sandi Masori

"My advice to planners, would be that if the venue says 'no balloons,' check if it's actually no helium rather than no balloons, because I have found that several venues that said they didn't want helium balloons, because of past issues that they had had. When I showed them a photo of an amazing sculpture that is air filled, and will never go to the ceiling, they didn't have a problem with that type of décor."

To touch on Quinceaneras a little, I've found that they are very much like a wedding in the décor that they use, with a lot of tulle and fluffy elements. Here are some pictures of a couple of my favorite Quinces.

Photo and Design by Sandi Masori

Photo and Design by Joette Giardina

Weddings

Photo and Design by Holland and Sean Muscio

While flowers are usually the go-to for wedding décor, don't discount the impact that balloons can make for weddings. They can either be fun and whimsical, or soft and beautiful. Combining balloons with tulle and lights is always a sure hit for weddings. I asked some of my balloon friends what trends they had been seeing in weddings, and if they had any advice for planners who were interested in using balloons for weddings. Here's what they had to say

Tammy: "We get a lot of people who are little apprehensive about doing balloons at their event. They think if there's going to be a lot of kids there; they're going to pop the balloons. I assure them that it's not usually the kids that pop the balloons; it's the drunk groomsmen that pop the balloons. Once they see some of the pictures of the work that we've done, they're a little more open to it. I can't sell every bride on balloons though. Those that do want balloons usually will take something on the dance floor, maybe a heart sculpture behind the head table, columns behind the cake table, and something at the entrance. It's really kind of difficult to get them to incorporate it into the centerpieces. I think they have a preconceived idea that it's going to be childlike, and they may not understand that they can be elegant and beautiful and really bring a lot to their event. I show them some of the things that we've done like Lomey bowls and vases. A lot of times these are more elegant; you can get some height to it. It may be that for the same budget you would spend on a little flower arrangement, you could spend the same amount with me, and you're going to get this huge centerpiece that's high in the air, that's going to get a lot of attention, and that's going to have that wow factor that those flowers just aren't going to have. So I try to compare us to a florist. Look at what you're going to get with a florist, and look what you'll get when you come to me. I just feel the balloons have such a big impact."

Steve: "The private events that I do with planners the most are weddings. Don't get me wrong, it's not a ton of them, but, especially nowadays, with the big popularity of the three footers being used at weddings; we're doing a lot of those. Every once in a while you're getting one or two that want to do something for the shower too. It's mostly classic décor, but I specialize in a lot of sculpture work, so it's not unusual for me to sell sculptures of the bride and groom to a wedding.

Photo and Design by Steve Jones

" The great thing about the three footers is that they are transportable. If a bride is on a budget they can be used in multiple locations throughout the event. They can stage them on the dance floor; they can stage them wherever they want them. They can put them at the head table then move them around. We've had several of them outside as well, for outdoor ceremonies and the like. We've had to remind them thought that there may be a problem is they want to take them from outside to inside. Latex reacts to the air and the light. So we try to encourage them to get two sets for inside and out."

Tammy: "The bridal table is typically the most important; that's where they want most of the focus. The cake table is another one that we usually highlight, usually something on the dance floor. Entrance décor, probably 50% of our events do entrance décor, not all of them will go for it. Centerpieces are of course important, getting the right size and style of centerpiece for the wedding, sometimes that's a little tricky because they have something in their head that want that may not necessarily work on the tables that they have, or in the venue."

Photo and Design by Joette Giardina

Steve: "The number one issue we run into with weddings is the element of customer service. When it comes to a wedding you absolutely have to be super attentive. You have to respond quickly to emails, you have to respond quickly to phone calls, because if you don't, well we all the bridezilla , groomzilla and momzilla concept. After getting married myself recently, I can relate to all of it. It's a very significant time in that person's life; it's a very significant event, and because of that they're walking around on pins and needles. Getting married recently gave me a really good approach to this, because it's easy to look at a bride as another client, but when you're that person, then you realize the magnitude of what you're putting together. It's like, 'oh wow.' It really did kind of change my perspective a little bit. If you're working with the event planners that don't normally work with balloons a lot, there's a lot of coordination I think that needs to take place with the venue. You need to make sure what their policies are, and other factors. There's nothing worse than booking a whole bunch of three foot balloons for a wedding, and then finding out they have laser based smoke detectors, and they don't allow helium balloons for that reason. So the biggest thing would be to know the venue. Also, the bride or the client is not always right. There's a lot of physics involved with balloons, for example, you get a call from people who want to hang a banner off a three foot balloon. They've got a ten foot banner; and they say, 'well we just want two three foot balloons to hold the banner up.' That's not going to work. So sometimes you need to explain why they can't have what they want."

Joette: "Nowadays it seems like most of my wedding décor is more of what people have found on Pinterest and with the fabric draping. We also have the occasional client that says they would really love to have a balloon drop at their first dance or at the end of the evening, or they would like a few columns and things like that. So it's kind of a mix."

Photo and Design by Sandi Masori

Joette: [For the planners that don't really consider balloons for weddings] "I'd say check out Pinterest, because I've been getting lots of calls recently to do three foot balloons from the ceiling or larger. I think what happens is that when the everyday person who doesn't know a lot about balloons looks at some of the photos and their sense of sizing may be off. They look at something, and they think it's a three foot balloon. For example, the client that just called me the other day said, 'oh I want you to put all these wonderful three foot balloons up for our wedding reception.' So then I went and looked at the pictures that she had pulled, and actually the smallest balloon in the picture was three foot, and the other ones were probably four, five, and six foot balloons. So I let her know, I said 'if you're going for that exact look that you're seeing on Pinterest you may not sure about the sizing, because you've probably never seen a balloon that big.' There's a hefty price tag that goes with purchasing that size of a balloon. I think that's the number one thing for people who are looking at doing their own balloons for their wedding, they don't know about

Photo and Design by Sandi Masori

professional balloons, and they don't know all the details of how long it takes to inflate a balloon, and everything that they need to know to install that to the space and how much time it would take. I've seen a lot of times where people have done balloons for their own wedding, and you walk in the door at 9:00 in the morning, and there's all these helium balloons blown up. And I ask the staff 'what time is this wedding reception?' And they're like 'it's at 6:00 tonight,' and I'm like 'oh, that's so sad, because the balloons they used were just nine inch balloons.' They were blowing them up at 8:00 in the morning, and you know that they were going to be on the floor before the reception even started. That's the sad part is when an event planner or an individual tries to do the balloons themselves, and they just don't know about all the details that go along with getting the balloons to last."

Dianna: "My first recommendation to any bride is if they are planning a wedding, don't worry about your dress as much as you need to worry about getting your event venue secured, and making sure that it's the right venue. You're going to spend money one way or the other. You're going to spend it for a really elaborate venue and you don't have to decorate, or you're going to spend it on a very plain venue like a National Guard Armory or a gym or something, and you'll spend your money on the décor. In regard to balloons, a lot of brides around here tend to do outside weddings, and outside weddings and balloons in East Tennessee don't do very well because of humidity and heat. So they need to factor that in. A lot of people think that all balloons have helium in them, and so they need to know that there are a whole lot of things that can be done with balloons that don't look chintzy or cheap, that they can look elegant."

Joette also shared a really unique wedding that she decorated...

Joette: "One that was unique was a wedding that asked to have seven foot tall sea horses at the entrance of their wedding. To me that was just kind of a unique thing because typically a lot of the weddings aren't asking for balloons, but they did, and they asked for sea horses. It turned out really cool."

Design and Photo by Tammy Corzine

Photo and Design by Holland and Sean Muscio

Advanced Balloons

Design by Sandi Masori
Photo by Gary Schacker

Sculptures, branded stages and special effects like balloon drops, releases and exploding balloons, can make big impact for any type of event, and are sure to have people talking. These are more advanced balloons and should be left in the hands of the experts though. Let's see what our balloon pros have to say about them...

Photo and Design by Dianna Glandon

Sculptures

Most serious balloon artists will do some sculptures at some point in their career. Sculptures are incredibly time consuming, but also traffic-stopping. I sat down with Tammy to talk about some of her sculptures.

Tammy: "I think the first one we had probably took about 20, 26, 28 hours. The ones that I've worked on at FLOAT were probably 36 to 40 hours. The build time is pretty fast. It goes together pretty quickly when we have a plan and everything. Now the planning process and sketching and trial and error, that takes a lot of man hours. We spend weeks on it drawing up designs and doing little mini mockups and things like that. The last couple big sculptures that I did I actually worked with someone who lived fairly close to me, so we would get together for meetings and try different things. A lot of things ended up on the floor, but what we took from it obviously did well. I would say it probably took close to 100 hours by the time you figure all the time we put into it.

"When we're planning these kind of projects, we try to come up with a theme, or if there is a theme that we have to go with, we kind of Google that and see what comes up. We look at artwork and photographs, and anything that we can, and try and get that feeling that we're going for. And with the frogs for example, while the design was fairly elaborate as far as the frogs themselves, the overall design was fairly simple. It was two reeds with two frogs on them. That was pretty much it, but it was all the little details that made it a winner; we gave the frogs expressions and emotions. That elicits the emotion in the people.

"Sometimes when I'm designing it starts with a technique that I've seen that I just fell in love with, and I say 'I have to use this somewhere,' and I build a sculpture around the technique that I wanted to use. Other times I've seen a painting or something that I thought, 'that's just beautiful. How can I do that in balloons?' The frogs were actually from a picture that my mom found that she thought was cool, and it was two frogs *(pictured in beginning of book)*. So that's kind of where we got that idea, but we can take any idea, and we translate it into balloons."

Photo and Design by Anne McGovern

Photo and Design by Steve Jones

Sculptures are useful as a photo op area, as a sponsorship opportunity for corporate events, as a focal point, or as a navigation device (as in it's the door by the mermaid). When people see life-size, or larger than life sculptures, not only does it call out to them, but people can't resist taking pictures with it. The reaction is really huge. Pictures don't do it justice, you really have to see it in person. But, until you have the opportunity to see it live, here are some pix...

Photo and Design by Sandi Masori

Photo and Design by Blenda Berrier

Photo and Design by Dianna Glandon

Photo and Design by Steve Jones

Photo and Design by Dianna Glandon

Photo and Design by Jill Shortreed

Drops, Releases
and Exploding Balloons

Photo and Design by Chris Potts

Nothing makes a point like special effects. Special effects would include balloon drops (where the balloons fall from a net on the ceiling down to the ground), balloon releases (where the balloons float from a net on the ground up to the air), and exploding balloons (where large balloons are filled with little balloons which are released when the outer balloon is popped).

I talked to Chris, Joette and Steve about their thoughts on drops and releases.

Chris: [Re Themed Drops] "Whenever there's a theme, again, a lot of times we do these Under the Sea themes, and then we'll drop instead of just regular balloons, we'll drop '260' creations (made from the long skinny balloons), or simple octopuses, and just fun things from the ceiling. We did a party just the other day with Under the Sea; we did all small little figurines, like sea horse, and octopuses, and fish in the drop. Within 30 seconds, every balloon was picked up and taken home; it was great."

Chris also spoke about the ceiling requirements for a good drop: "Say they want a drop, but the ceiling's only 10 feet tall. The net is three feet deep, which means that the bottom of the net is only seven feet off the ground, so if you're standing underneath it and you're six foot tall there's only one foot between you and the bag, and that doesn't give the balloons a chance to disperse and look great throughout the air. So you try to talk them out of it, and they get a little disappointed, but you don't want to sell them something just to get the money. You have to have it look good, or it's just very odd. That's when we would, again, try to lean them towards the streamer launches that could be handheld and work great in a 10 foot ceiling, the confetti launches. I would say that the minimum ceiling height for a drop would be 12 feet."

Joette had this advice for planners who are interested in drops:

Joette: "When you plan to use a balloon drop as a key special effect, timing is important

It's very important for the person who is pulling the line to know the schedule of events and details of things happening leading up to the drop. NYE is typically an easy cue - count down from 10 to 1....But at an awards ceremony, or product reveal - depending on the size of a drop advance knowledge of the program is needed. An awards night, for example,....let the rigger know what the last 3 awards will be and come up with a line to say to cue the drop. Also, have the MC prepared to say something as the drop is being pulled.

"Depending on the size of the drop, and the amount of line that is 'out from bag' to where the line is being pulled, there can be a delay when the drop is being pulled to bring in the slack etc. Make sure to prep the MC in advance so that they say what they are supposed to say to give the cue.... And prep the MC that if there is a delay they should just keep interacting with the audience rather than just sitting quietly, looking up to the sky, waiting for the balloons to drop."

Personally, I prefer to sell exploding balloons over drops. The exploding balloons are jumbo balloons filled with little 5' balloons- about 150- 200 in each one. They go up on the ceiling, and get taken for granted as part of the décor. Then, when the cue is given, we hit the button to pop the balloon and all the little balloons come cascading down. No matter how fancy the audience, it always goes straight into a balloon stomp after that. The exploders are detonated by electrical impulse, so it's not pyrotechnic. It always gets a great reaction. We do them for NYE, of course, but also for corporate events for a big reveal or to rally people. Also, they're really popular for Bar Mitzvahs as well.

Photo and Design by Sandi Masori

Design by Sandi Masori
Photo by Gary Schacker

Now let's talk about balloon releases. Every city has different ordinances on balloon releases. Here in San Diego, you need to notify the FAA if the release will be over 25 balloons. Also, most of the city is in the flight path, so we have a lot of restrictions on heights and things going up in the air.

Photo and Design by Chris Potts

Both Chris and Steve had some words of wisdom on balloon releases.

Chris: "Well, you always want to use a balloon that's 100% biodegradable, and you don't want to put any ribbons or things on the balloons. We're not talking about releasing 100,000 balloons like they do for the Indianapolis 500. Usually it's just a few hundred to a few thousand, so you don't have to do too much. There's not any permission here in New York state that you have to get. I used to call the airport and let them know, and they were like why you calling me? The balloons just disperse in the air, and they're 100% biodegradable, which is a great thing."

Though Chris' experience in upstate New York is that releases are not an issue, and the FAA doesn't need to be notified, Steve found otherwise on the west coast.

Steve: "We did a release at my own wedding, we actually got married in Oregon, in a public park overlooking Cannon Beach. In Oregon they have litter laws; but the litter laws specifically exclude balloons, so balloon releases are 100% okay. Oregon is a very environmentally conscious state, so the fact that they exclude balloons, shows that they're not an environmental problem.

"The only thing I really, really wanted to do at the wedding was a balloon release, because we're going to be on this bluff, and it's going to be fun. And everybody's going to enjoy it, and have a really nice time. And I have to say it was the most perfect balloon release I've ever done. The wind stopped; I mean stopped. The balloons went straight up.

"It was beautiful; it was perfect, but a park employee, 10 minutes before the wedding was to begin, openly bawled at me, like cried at me, 'how dare I!' I mean we'd been working together all day, because I was doing all the setup for the wedding. My wife was getting ready; I was moving the chairs, setting up, working with the tent people and doing all that stuff. Coordinating all the logistics of the actual set up, and she was openly crying. "I've been working with you all day, you're so nice; you're so respectful, and I can't believe you would do this to the environment.'

"I shared with her the information that I had. And of course then she encouraged me to go to all these websites that are trashing the industry, and the whole bit. I was like, 'okay, I think we're just going to respectfully agree to disagree.' I did verify this; I checked it out, called everybody involved; I'm okay.

"In Seattle we've had similar situations. We had a balloon release for a big church event here, and it was 1,600 balloons. We verified that it was perfectly legal, it was not in violation of anything else. We even called the airport and let them know, and they actually created a four mile no- fly zone during the time frame.

"Here in Seattle, there are a ton of commuter flights, little prop planes, and sea planes that take off all the time, and fly around the area. Yeah, they just decided during that time frame to create a four mile no fly zone around the city so that the balloon release could go off and not affect anybody. Because a thick balloon release can bring down a Cessna. In fact, I interviewed, Senator Jack Scott, the California state senator who was actually responsible for the attempted ban on foil balloons.

"I was trying to get a feel for where he was coming from, and one of his fellow state senators said that he couldn't wait to vote to ban the balloons because he owns a Cessna, and he actually got caught up in a balloon release once, and almost crashed his plane. It was almost like he had a vendetta to settle.

Design by Steve Jones

"So there's a lot of things that need to be considered. If you're doing a balloon release of any size, a responsible decorator's going to contact the local airport and let them know that what's going to happen."

I would definitely recommend that you contact a balloon professional when planning a release. They will either know the local rules, or have the resources to quickly find them out.

Photo and Design by Blenda Berrier

Stages

Photo and Design by Sandi Masori

Stages are one of my very favorite things to do. I see so many stages that depend on lights to set the mood, and while it looks great, it doesn't photograph well or get into the photos. Doing a branded balloon wall you can still use the light effects to make it more interesting or upscale, but when the lights are off, it's still a great set. People love taking pictures of and with the speakers, and those photos have a tendency to end up online. I've done some sets where years later the speakers are still using the picture as their profile photo, because it's so branded, and so obvious that it's a big stage.

It's important that the colors on the stage don't show too many shadows, or mess with the color balance for the cameras (for events that will be recorded). It's also important the décor or balloons don't move or distract from the speaker. They should enhance and frame the speakers, not take away.

Stage décor doesn't have to be elaborate to be effective. On the budget side of things, a couple of columns on either side of the stage can be really effective. If there is a little bit more of a budget, then five-seven columns can work really well. Two columns should be at the front of the stage, flanking it, and three to five columns (depending on the length of the stage) should be on the back of the stage. If you have a really good budget, then nothing beats the impact of a full-size branded balloon stage wall.

Jessie, a planner who specializes in multi-day, multi-speaker events had this to say about using balloons as a stage backdrop;

Jessie: "I know we have used some helium balloons or ones that float around on the outside, but anything that is going to be on camera or on stage always needs to be somehow very stationary so there's no movement at all. We never want people to be distracted and taken away from what the speaker's saying on stage.

"I would say probably my favorite balloon experience was the very first time we had a whole balloon wall, because I just thought it looked really cool on camera. The way it photographed for stills and on camera just gave this like texture to the stage that I hadn't seen

Photo and Design Sandi Masori

before. You typically, when you go to these multi-speaker events, you'll see the traditional pipe and drape in the background, and this just added this new dimension and texture to what we did.

"And that kind of blew me away, so we since then have done a lot with those balloon walls and the custom logo or sign in the middle. I love that. And then I also really, really love when we did, you know I don't what the terminology is, but it almost looked like a street stand. It had those big giant light-up balloons on the top that they'd put a light through, so it kind of looked like a street stand. And to me that was really cool too, because I hadn't seen it done. I always like just something different and unique is what appeals to me." *(I call them balloon lamps)*

Design Sandi Masori
Photo Debbie LeFever

Photo and Design by Chris Potts

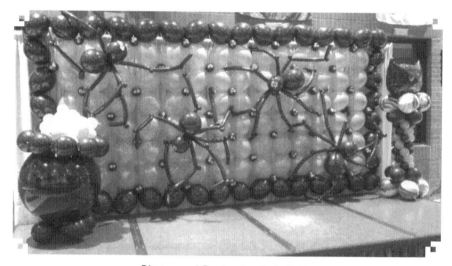

Photo and Design by Chris Potts

Design by Sandi Masori
Photo by Debbie LeFever

Corporate Events

Photo and Design by Dianna Glandon

Photo and Design by Sandi Masori

Trade Shows and Conferences

Photo and Design by Chris Potts

Tradeshows and conferences are my favorite kind of events. So much so that I wrote an entire book about them! There are several ways that balloons can help at these events:

• Navigation

• Focal Points

• Sponsorship Opportunities

• Carrying Messages/ Lead generation and management

• Branding

These are not mutually exclusive. The balloons that are used for navigation can also carry the branding. Often conferences are at really large venues or convention centers where there are multiple events at the same time, or multiple tracks from the same event. Using colorful balloon décor can help people easily spot the areas that belong to that event, or that track. Branding can be accomplished by imprinted balloons, custom art work made from foamboard, printed signs, balloon sculptures or logos, or large 3-d mascots. Whenever you can also turn that into a photo op area with unique pieces, you're more likely to see those photos showing up in social media during and after the event.

Stages are another great place to bring in the branding. Using a stage wall backdrop made from balloons can bring in some incredi-

Photo and Design by Sandi Masori

ble color and texture to what otherwise likely would have just been the plain wall of the venue, or the same pipe and drape as every other event.

Jessie, a planner who does a lot of conferences, said "we've done these really elaborate sets, where the whole backdrop is basically built out of a balloon wall, and then we'll have the logo, a custom made sign, hanging in the middle, and then we typically have balloons in registration area, and kind of around the room to frame the rooms and key points such as like the sales table, or just to keep it consistent and the same colors and branding throughout the room."

At tradeshows, using colorful columns, not only to direct traffic, but also to carry messages can put those messages right up at eye level. A great way to use those signs and messages is to use a text based messaging system. The signs direct people to text in their name and email for updates. Then throughout the event, you can send those messages directly to people's cell phones- messages like: "the speak-

Photo and Design by Sandi Masori

er in ballroom A is starting 15 minutes late", or "come back to the main ballroom for the raffle" , or "breakout sessions starting in 15 minutes in ballrooms b,c and d".

As an exhibitor, using columns that are integrated with marketing messages can increase the number and quality of leads you get. The signs on the balloons direct people to opt into your list- either to enter a contest, which is the best way to get opt ins, or to get some sort of "ethical bribe" or swag. There are many systems out there, but the one that I use allows you to have an interactive text conversation with your prospects, so that you can qualify them, and then will also send out a follow up email. This means that you only need to call the hottest prospects.

Here's an example *(follow the directions in bold to see live example)*: -

Text your
NAME and EMAIL
to 858 207 4855

Photo and Design by Sandi Masori

You'll get a couple of text messages back. The first one is a verification text. In September 2013 new laws were passed that govern how you do text message marketing. One of those rules was that even if people opt in via text, they still have to confirm that they want to get messages from you.

After you text back that you agree to receive messages, there will be two interactive questions. Then there will be an immediate follow up

Photo and Design by Steve Jones

via e-mail. All of these things are happening automatically. It's an amazingly powerful system. Here's a link to a video that will tell you more about it: http://marketwithballoons.com/trade-show-total-marketing-packages

As far as using balloons for a sponsorship opportunity go, who wouldn't want to stop and take pictures with a fabulous sculpture, or sit on a life-size balloon motorcycle? Add the sponsor branding to the piece and you can sell them to help fund the event.

Yet one more place that balloons help with conferences is with keeping butts in the seats. When the ambiance inside the general session room is fun and inviting, there's more energy in the room, and people are more likely to stay in their seats, or return to the main session room after breaks.

Design by Sandi Masori
Photo by Jessica Price

A fun way to bring up the energy in a room is with jumbo 3' balloons. Have your balloon artist stuff them with a note for a prize. Don't tell anyone that's what's going on, and then when that 3:00 drowsiness takes over the crowd, turn up the music, throw the 3' balloons out into the crowd and they will bounce them back and forth. When the music stops, tell whoever is holding the jumbo balloon to pop it (it will be loud) and to take the prize note to the back of the room to claim their prize. Your next speaker will enjoy a much more energetic audience.

Photo and Design by Sandi Masori

Design by Sandi Masori
Photo by Debbie LeFever

If you want to know more about using balloons for trade shows and conferences, pick up a copy of my book *The Ultimate Guide To Inflating Your TradeShow Profits.... With Balloons!* – available on Amazon.

Photo and Design by Sandi Masori

Photo and Design by Sandi Masori

Grand Openings

Grand openings are a perfect time to use balloons. Often people just think, "ok I'm doing a grand opening so I need an arch." But I always like to ask, "what are you trying to accomplish?" If your goal is to attract attention from afar, maybe columns at the door, and ground clusters leading up to the store will attract attention and draw people in.

Photo and Design by Jill Shortreed

Inside the store on the other hand, maybe you want to call attention to certain aisles or promotions- so you may want to put some helium balloons there, or if you have high ceilings, then maybe put some sort of hanging décor. This is actually a place that a spiral arch could make sense as well- a traditional spiral arch leads the eye up and over, so if you want to highlight two promo aisles, this can be really effective.

The other thing that I always ask about is lead generation- it's not enough just to get people into the store- what you really want is to have them come back again and again. So we will often package the balloons with a SMS based lead generation solution- people can opt themselves in by texting to a unique phone number posted around the store. The best motivators to get people to join the list are either a contest, or an instant give-away. Then you can draw those people back to the store again and again.

Studies show that people are never more than 3 feet away from their phones and that every text message gets looked at. The real trick is to make sure that you are delivering value with every touch. So if you have a slow day in the store, you can send out a text blast saying 'first 50 people to come in get x', or something like that. And for a grand opening, those signs, inviting people to enter the contest, or get the instant give-away, should be integrated right into the décor- up on the columns at the entrance, or on the promo aisle arches. At the register the cashiers should be reminding people, but the signs should be everywhere too.

This way, maybe they are attracted in by the balloons, and maybe they don't buy anything that day, but you're communicating with them every so often, so the next time they might buy. Otherwise, you might attract them in the first time, but if you don't capture their info, you have no way to bring them back in. So you end up spending more money on advertising to bring in more new customers instead of making more money from the existing customers. Also, having monthly or seasonal promotions and displays can keep people coming in again and again. They'll want to see what you've done now. So they'll keep coming back to see the new display.

Here's an example of a texting campaign *(follow the directions in bold)*:

Text your
NAME and EMAIL
to 858 207 4855

See the chapter on trade shows to learn more about this type of lead generation.

Photo and Design by Blenda Berrier

Now, let's talk more about decorating for the grand opening. Planners Julie, Jessie and balloon pro Jill were gracious enough to share their thoughts on grand openings with me.

Julie: "The events that we specialize in and do majority of are grand opening events. So for us, and our clients, balloons are very important. We typically use the balloons outside, and our main purpose for balloons is for our drive by traffic. So we love balloons.

"My best story is just the continued success that we have today, and what I mean by that, our order is not that large, but it's extremely important to our client, and what we have in place today is a very good model, and it works for our client. These balloons do go outside, and our main purpose to have these balloons in having these balloons is to attract people and let them know that 'we're now open', and to come in and see what it's all about. We all feel that it's very successful, what we're doing today. We do have some restrictions and permits that prohibit us from putting balloons out in certain areas, certain cities, that sort of thing. When we don't have balloons, they do not have the traffic; we know that. So we try to have balloons everywhere. We do risk permitting sometimes, but it is on a case by case basis, and the reason we do that is because we know it works. I think that it's really a significant increase in foot traffic. We don't have that data to back it up, but from word of mouth and from the client-- they're happy, so that makes me say yes.

"That is primarily the only use of balloons that we're doing. Probably 95% of our business is grand openings. We specialize in high volume openings, in a year's time frame we will do 250 to 500 events a year. Our grand openings are very important to us, and that's where we mainly do our balloons. I've been doing this for this client for about 11 years, and we started out doing latex balloons, and doing arches and columns, and like I mentioned, they always went outside. Then, a couple years ago we switched over to foil balloons, and we really love the foil balloons. It was something different. We started using these foil balloons, not only in columns, but in ground pole clusters. That just gave it just a little bit more, something different, something unique to balloons. I feel like because of all of the education from the balloon partners that we have across the country, I now know a little bit about latex and foil balloons."

Photo and Design Sandi Masori

Jessie added these words of wisdom...

Jessie: " I'll see a lot of balloons used at events, grand openings, birthday parties, or galas, and it amazes me that they don't stay consistent with what their colors are. A lot of what I do with my clients is try to get them to focus on how they want to be branded, and I like to see one to three colors maximum at an event, in a business, on a logo, or on a website. Anything more just gets too busy. I think a lot of businesses miss the mark, let's say when they're having a grand opening, and their colors are blue and yellow. They should only have their balloons be blue and yellow. Why are they having every color of the rainbow? To me it makes it inconsistent, so that's where I feel like people miss the mark a lot with balloons."

Jill told me about some of the décor that she finds is most popular and effective for grand openings.

Jill: "Event Poles, They're air filled; I guess about 90% of what we do, maybe 95% of what we do, is air filled. We use coordinating ribbons down off the bottom, so you get some movement without having the

Photo and Design Jill Shortreed

helium balloons, so they're going to flutter in the wind. They're kind of like a partial column with a topper, and we either drive them in the ground, or we attach them to some sort of structure or fencing, bleacher, something along those lines. We do quite of bit of them; we've done them for builders. We just did them for a physician's office that had a patient appreciation; they wanted to draw attention from the street. They were on a highway. They're usually eight feet. So they draw a nice attention, but like I said, it just really depends on the installation. We can do them as small as five feet, but that doesn't have as much of an impact as the eight footers do.

Photo and Design Jill Shortreed

"There's the branding aspect, that you're using the corporate colors. We did one recently that was for a children's center, and we replicated their logo in balloons. They had the Chamber of Commerce, the press, and the mayor and other dignitaries there. It blew her mind that we were able to actually replicate her logo. It took center stage for her ribbon cutting, and it stayed there all day. So it adds to that whole fun atmosphere, and the whole branding aspect of what balloons can do for them. They attracted attention from everybody who was driving by, because if you're driving by and you see balloons, naturally you're going to take a look as to what's going on.

"My background, and my education is in marketing and finance, so that kind of helps with my clients as far as being able to recommend the balloons and connect it to the marketing aspect. When we do our nonprofits, or any client that's doing a grand opening, we always tweet about it, and we post it on Facebook to try to drive extra traffic to them, giving the client added exposure. It's just included in what we do, and as far as the financing part of my background, I think that helps, because we keep them on their budget, and don't let them over spend, and if they are going to push their budget limits, we can justify why we're going to up the budget.

"We can also do the ribbon service for them. I would definitely tell them to call the mayor's office and the Chamber of Commerce to try to get some dignitaries there, for their publicity shoots. I tell them that the balloons will be excellent backdrop to that. We can provide the ribbon to coordinate with the balloon décor so they actually have a nice ribbon to cut. It's all about marketing, and press releases, and making people aware. You're just not buying balloons from me; you're buying the atmosphere. You're buying the marketing aspect of it. It's just not pretty balloons on a string."

When I asked Jill what advice she had for planners doing grand openings she warned about the challenges of balloons outside.

Jill: "Often clients will call for grand openings and ask for a balloon arch; 'how much is a balloon arch?' Balloon arches do not always work very well around here, because of the expansion of helium and we tend to get very windy here. If a client insists on an arch, and it is too windy, we might make the executive decision to split it into columns for you."

I was curious what her favorite grand opening was. This was what she shared...

Jill: "We did Jet Blue when they landed here. Actually we did Southwest and Jet Blue, when they both landed here in Charleston, and that was one of my favorite ones too, because we made little airplanes for the counters, and all the other airlines walked up, and they were like 'this is so cool. Why didn't we get those?' Jet Blue even tweeted about the balloons, which was cool. We also did giant blue palm trees for them, and blue and white columns all throughout the airport. We do a lot of those product launches. We also have another large company here, who unfortunately has to call us at the last minute, because they're a software launching company, and they can't release their stuff ahead of time. We usually only get 24 to36 hours, if we're lucky on those events. For one of their events, they called us

Photo and Design Jill Shortreed

at 6:00 on a Friday night for an 8:00am install of five arches and six columns in their corporate colors. We keep a heavy stock, so we were actually able to pull that off for them."

Photo and Design by Holland Muscio

Photo and Design Sandi Masori

Photo and Design by Chris Potts

Sports Events

Sporting events are another place where balloons can have huge impact. It's hard to decorate stadiums and large places in ways that will make a difference. I sat down with Holland and Chris to learn more about the types of décor and challenges that you would see at sports events.

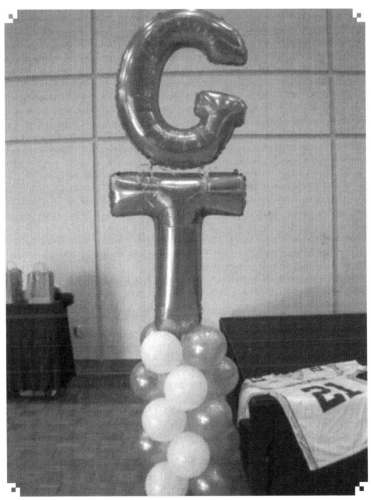

Photo and Design Holland and Sean Muscio

Holland: "Our largest client is Georgia Tech Athletics, so we work hand in hand with the Athletic Department, particularly during the football and basketball seasons to help decorate the facilities in gold and white balloons. During football season we're out there every game day; we've got columns and arches that we put up all around the stadium that end up going into the stadium, and the players run out under the arches onto the field. That's a very long time relationship that we've been able to continue and be a part of. Then during basketball season we do some similar band day experiences, and just help them make it a festive experience. We do a lot of football player sculptures, or basketball player sculptures, that look really nice as you walk into an event. We do a lot of monogramming of the jerseys, like during the SEC tournament that has come into town for years, and Dr. Pepper has hired us, and we'll do a football player and put the Dr. Pepper logo on the jersey of the sculpture. We've made the basketball goal, and then there's just classic décor that they like to use, because balloons go really well with sporting events. It's just something people associate together. Also I like to use the fireworks columns of the 260s because they kind of look like pom-poms."

Chris: "The Sabers are a great client, and we always do their home opener every year. They want us to decorate the foyer in the arena, which is a huge space. Every year, they'll pick out things, last couple of years they've got these giant cement columns that have a six foot diameter column and are 30 feet high. We wrap them all in balloons, and they love it. We'll do their logo out of balloons, which is a big circular ring with Saber swords through the center of it. So we'll make giant logos. Everything that we do, since it's such a high ceiling, a big venue, will be big. So it's big logos, big swags, and just covering the columns; it's not a lot of tricky stuff, mostly classic balloon décor. In the last two years they were both just supposed to be for the home opener, and they loved it so much that asked to keep it up for the next game. Sometimes the next game is three, four days away, and the good thing about doing all of this stuff, is that it's all air filled décor. With just a couple of balloons being refreshed on the day of the next event we can have an event that will last four days. They'll have it through two games, so they get a better value out of it. The planner didn't even know balloons could last that long, so they're just amazed that things can look so good four days later. Those are great clients to work with. Those are a lot of fun, working in the arenas.

Photo and Design Chris Potts

Photo and Design Chris Potts

Photo and Design Chris Potts

Photo and Design by Chris Potts

Upscale

Design by Sandi Masori
Photo by Doug Gates

There are many ways to make balloons fit with a high-end or upscale event. The first thing that comes to my mind is lights, lights and lights. Also, using different lines, high contrast colors, and lots of foil balloons will make for a very elegant effect. Tammy and Dianna also had something to say on the topic.

Tammy: "We did an 80th birthday party. They just wanted something bright and fun, so we used multicolored tablecloths. Every table was a different color; we just did bouquets of four or five balloons, but in those bright colors that matched the tablecloths, the use of color in that event was very effective.

"When a planner comes to me and says that they want to use balloons for a high end event, I would suggest showing some of the things that we've done with foil balloons, the tapers and the curves and the crescents, the designs that you can create with that, sculptures, and ceiling dangles. There are just some really awesome designs you can do that are not childish, and are very upscale."

Photo and Design by Tammy Corzine

Photo and Design by Tammy Corzine

Photo and Design by Tammy Corzine

Photo and Design by Dianna Glandon

Dianna: "A lot of times we'll suggest combining something like a three foot balloon on top of a column that has some fabric below it, and then do some up lighting. Because the three foot balloon will really fill the space, we can put lighting on it and it shines around the whole room and gives more of an elegant feel. So many people dim their rooms completely, so we often will say, 'Let us do white balloons and put light on them.' Lighting companies love it because they like to bounce the colors off of the balloons. If they are white or clear balloons, they love them. So if they want a more elegant look, we almost always suggest the larger balloons with some fabric in it."

Photo and Design Jill Shortreed

Photo and Design Joette Giardina

Photo and Design Sandi Masori

Photo and Design by Tammy Corzine

Big Venues - Galas

Photo and Design Chris Potts

Some of the most fun events to decorate are the galas and big venues, like large ballrooms or what have you. Steve, Dianna, Joette and Chris had a lot to say about these events.

Steve says that coordination between vendors is really important.

Steve: "Large scale, sales oriented, meetings and sales functions tend to be internal events versus marketing events. Larger companies hire the event planner to come in and coordinate a special event that's taking place internally, and that's what we end up doing more of than anything. We're working with a florist, we're working with a caterer, we're working with AV people. We're all coordinating this together.

"In most cases it's the event planner that's doing all of that coordination, but every once in a while, especially when you work with the same people all the time, and you know the venue, you know that the freight elevator's only so big, and you know that you can call the other vendors and see when they're going to arrive, so that you can make sure that you're not all pulling up to the loading dock at the same time."

Joette also mentioned that a key to success is coordination between the vendors.

Joette: "When I'm working with an awards banquet that may be 1,000 people, typically we go into the venue the day before. We want to be able to go in there and put things in the space, and see when the people are coming in for the sound checks and the tech for all the different entertainment that might be going on to make sure none of the décor that we have set up is in their way. And it can get moved a little bit if needed.

"Many of the corporate events that I do either have a number of people up on stage, or have live performances going on where there's several stage changes throughout the evening. So you just want to

Photo and Design by Joette Giardina

make sure that that décor is set appropriately not to be in anyone's way. A lot of times those events are being filmed live; you want to make sure nothing is blocking the camera shot.

"Typically with a larger event, I like to go in the day before, so that I can work out a lot of those details, and then on the day of the event when we're sitting there the tech rehearsals are going on, everything's in place, and it's easy to get things taken care of."

Dianna shared that her favorite corporate events were the galas and explained a bit about what she likes to do for them and the trends and challenges that she has seen.

Dianna: My favorite corporate events would be the ones where they let me do the entire ballroom, and I do the centerpieces, and I pull the full room together. I'll call it more of a gala, or a big banquet, those are the ones that are my favorite because then I'm actually able to showcase the power of balloons and how they can paint the air with color, and how it makes a tremendous impact on their event. For example, we did an event where they were celebrating the 65th anniversary of this organization, and they were also doing it as a fundraiser. They had asked us to do some balloon décor, and I convinced them to let me do stuff from the ceiling of this massive ballroom. We put lights on it, and then we did the entrance décor. Now even after three years, people will still see me and they will say, 'oh my gosh. I remember when you did this', but more than anything, they ended up raising more money that night than they had ever raised.

"To me, it's because of a very subconscious effect that balloons have, and that is, 'Wow. You really care about me. You made me happy, therefore I'm in a happy mood, therefore I feel more generous.' People don't understand that that's what happens, but I firmly believe it is because I've seen it happen numerous times.

"We have made chandeliers that are ten feet in diameter that have lights on them, blinking. We have hung tall classic columns from the ceiling and had them spin. We've draped fabric. We have done three foot balloons coming from the table, chandelier kind of things, and then usually some stage décor with that, and some arches outside. We've done different balloon drops too. People like balloon drops because they're fun, but I feel like you're spending a lot of money on a balloon drop for a few seconds of fun, and that it would be better if you make the whole room look better the whole time.

Photo and Design by Dianna Glandon

"I think if you're in a big room, like with a thirty foot ceiling, you need to consider the ceiling as an integral part of your room décor. When we put balloons on the ceiling, meaning hanging balloons from the ceiling, or fabric, then what that does is it lowers the ceiling and creates a more intimate atmosphere. To me, hanging something from the ceiling, lowering the ceiling, or bringing something large up from the ceiling is far more important than anything else you do. I think setting a welcoming entrance is important, but I don't think they should spend the brunt of their money on the entrance because you walk through and you're done.

"I would want to know what kind of atmosphere they want. Do they want a classic kind of atmosphere, or do they want fun or whimsical? Do they want formal? That would be kind of hard. If they were on a limited budget, and they let's say they're in a ceiling that's sixteen feet or higher, which means we can do anything we want. I would probably tell them to go with very simple style décor. I really try to stay away from balloons on a string because I don't think that it is creative, but sometimes that's a really effective way to fill your room with color. It sets a good atmosphere. Now I wouldn't do just a balloon on a string so much as maybe say, let's do a sixteen inch balloon and do something on it, or maybe create a giant flower and float it, or something like that. I always try to do air filled décor be-

Photo and Design by Chris Potts

cause I think your money goes further. A lot of times, if I have some-body with a limited budget, I say, 'Are you guys going to do your cen-terpieces or do you want us to do it?' They'll say, 'We're going to do it.' I'll say, 'Well then let's spend your money on the stage, or let's make a photo backdrop. People seem to like that, because if they have a limited budget they usually tend to have a good group of vol-unteers, and they like to make their own centerpieces."

Chris shared his experience working in venues with 100 foot ceilings, like sports arenas and the like.

Chris: "We do a lot of work with the local sports teams, with the Buf-falo Bills, the Buffalo Sabers. We do a lot of their events, and those are really fun, because the venues that they're in are quite large. The Bills have a practice facility that's bigger than the football field. The ceiling is probably 100 foot high.

"We're not rigging anything, because the ceiling's too high, but to fill that space, instead of making eight foot tall columns we make 20

Photo and Design by Chris Potts

foot tall columns. Instead of using 11 inch balloons, we use three foot balloons. They always want a real big impact; they've got a lot of room to fill. These are just great events that we get a chance to do for the Bills. They always want to come up with something special.

"It's exciting to be on the field with the players, and we've done balloon releases, a few times, when they're announcing new jerseys, new uniforms; we'll be on the field with big nets of 2-3,000 balloons, releasing them."

Design and Photo by Chris Potts

Joette also shared the décor that she most recommends for large events

Joette: "With corporate events, you're usually looking at several hundred people going into a space, so that typically means you're going to end up being in a large space that's pretty boring or dull. You want to be able to utilize a high quality balloon professional that can go into that space and transform it to make it something special.

"Based on a client's budget, what that means is that you want to do something towards the stage, because that's where your awards ceremony typically is taking place and your photos are being done. Find a balloon professional that can make something outstanding and crisp, that looks good in pictures, for your stage area.

"You also want to be able to create something special as people walk in the doors, whether that be something small out in the hallway to announce what's going on, maybe something really cool and amazing as they first walk in to get them excited about the evening's event. To me those are the two key areas to focus on at the beginning of a corporate event.

"A lot of times our corporate clients really like to have what I call a sculpted garland column, where it's not just super big balloons, but it's the larger balloons going down to smaller, back to larger, and then at the top maybe having a star or a three foot balloon, sometimes they may put their logo on that so it's something specialized and custom for them.

"And what they like about the columns is that it's something that doesn't move. It's something on a framework, so if you are having a

Photo and Design by Blenda Berrier

lot of people walk by it, or you have air conditioning vents, or doors being opened, the balloons won't be affected; they'll stay still and look great throughout the program. So that typically is one of the things that's requested the most."

Design by Dianna Glandon

Photo and Design by Sandi Masori

Photo and Design by Blenda Berrier

Photo and Design by Sandi Masori

Non- Profits

Balloons are great for non-profit events, and as Sherry, Chris and Blenda explain, can even help the event make money. Sherry, a professional auctioneer and auction consultant had a lot of interesting insights into the ways balloons can be used for auctions.

Sherry: "I think that there are a lot of creative ways to utilize balloons, and I think that maybe there is an imagery out there, and I mentioned this in the blog that some people have a thought that it's a little kids sort of thing, and certainly it can be. But I think like with a lot of things, even with auctions, people go in perhaps with a preconceived idea of what it is, but then once you start to get a little scratch under the surface you realize wow, this goes a lot deeper than what even I realized; there's a lot more things there that we can take advantage of that I didn't even know existed.

"Certainly I see that when people start talking to me about auctions, and I suspect that the same would be true with you and balloons, that there's lots of ways to utilize balloons. There are lots of different balloons out there, and it doesn't have to be for a seven year old's birthday party. It can be something that's very elegant and majestic, and lends an air or an aura of sophistication to an event that just hasn't been done before.

"Balloons are utilized in ways that you might not even be familiar with in an auction capacity. And let me just put some context to that. When we're talking about a benefit auction, there are some things we do from a standpoint of marketing, and some things that we do from a standpoint of maybe making it easy for the volunteers to collect money, for instance.

"There are a number of processes that we try to institute that are generally in place for reasons that might be obvious to the goer. So, one of those is actually utilizing balloons in a marketing capacity in a silent auction. A live auction is when we're actually physically calling the number. In that case the auctioneer's at the front of the room, and it's like hey, down, let's go, want to bid $100. I got $100 bid, around 50, what about a $150? That's a live auction, an oral auction, it's an actual environment where you're bidding live.

"But a silent auction, which are very popular in a benefit setting, is where there is a bid sheet, or it can be done electronically, but for the purposes of illustration let's just say there's a bid sheet down on a table, and people are writing their bid, hence the word silent. There's no actual call of the number increment, and so in a silent auction you may have 100 items out there that people are walking around and bidding on.

"One of the marketing techniques that help to drive revenue is that we call attention to items that are underbid or don't have bids. We may divide up that room into three sections, say a red section, a white section, and the blue section. Well, if we're closing the red section first, and they have some items that don't have bids, I'm going to be on that microphone talking to people.

Photo and Design by Anne McGovern

"I'll say, 'ladies and gentlemen, come over here to the red section, my gosh we've got a great deal. I know you're going to take your kids to Disneyland this year, or Disneyworld. I know you're going to that; they've got a great package here for $400. Come over, red balloons. Come over, red balloons. Come over,' and we're doing that because the balloons are high enough, if you make them high enough; I guess that's the first tip that you need a balloon that's eight feet high.

"But it's to draw attention, because it's a visual, device to get people to come over. It's easier than signage really; you can see it from all four directions. It's not like a sign which you can only see from the front. So balloons are utilized in that capacity for marketing, to direct people. 'Head towards the blue balloons. We're in the white section, look for the white balloons.'

"And I have countless photos on my site, and could even send you others, of balloons being utilized in that capacity when allowed. Sometimes hotels won't allow them, or a venue won't allow them, but wherever we can use them I say that's the easiest way, and the most effective way to utilize a balloon for marketing capacity.

"The other way that I've seen it utilized is in décor in general. So, for instance, there was a wonderful benefit auction that I did that was a political campaign rally, but not for any particular party. That was just the theme of the event, so they had red, white, and blue balloons in an archway. They had red, white and blue balloons over here; they had red, white, and blue balloons over there.

"And it was just to kind of help direct people into certain areas. So if you were in this section it kind of segued off the silent auction, here's the registration area, walk through this archway and you get to the ballroom. So that was a décor element that was more generic.

"Other ways that I've seen balloons used are in centerpieces, and I've see two ways that these are utilized. One way that I've seen, which I recently wrote a blog post about is utilizing the balloons on high strings so they don't interfere with the visibility, because that could be a big issues for an auctioneer. Visibility is a huge issue for auctions. You got to have the strings high enough, because that can be a very real thing.

"Now, that's no different than dealing with a centerpiece that is solid, like a big plastic leaf or something that you can't see through, but nonetheless, at least a balloon you can put on a string and get it high enough that it's not going to interfere, if you think that far ahead. So I've seen those as centerpieces, which looked really elegant. But then I've also seen uninflated balloons stretched over frames to make them look like flowers? *[They're called fantasy flowers.]* So we could use fantasy flowers, I've seen those as centerpieces too, which looked really nice, and hey, if you're afraid of people not liking the smell of

Photo and Design by Sandi Masori

real flowers, maybe they're allergic or something like that, or you don't want the things to die. Maybe you're doing it over the course of four or five days at a convention, and you want to keep things looking fresh, fantasy flowers ain't a bad way to go.

"Then, other ways they can be used, I'm going to go with the best example, starting out with the one that I wrote this blog post about, because that was the one that I had not seen before. They were using oversized balloons, I'm going to guess three to four feet ...[They're 36 inches], oversized balloons, and I think that was most interesting about it is first they weren't using a lot of balloons. I mean, maybe it was two balloons per every other table. So it didn't take that many balloons to have an impact, given that they were oversized. And the fact that they were oversized gave a much more elegant appeal to the entire environment than what you might see with smaller balloons. That's not to say there's not a place for smaller balloons though.

Photo and Design by Anne McGovern

"It tended to lower the ceiling of the ballroom, creating kind of a false ceiling effect, and very similar to the whole majestic or elegant quality that you might have if you were watching the hot air balloons rise on a desert summer in Phoenix for the wine festival. It's just this 'ah' feeling to it with the elegance of those balloons. And the color was nice, they were using various shades of pink, but I could see that you would have a similar feel to it if you were using other colors as well. I think that was probably the best experience I've seen with the balloons and how they were utilized.

"I don't have a lot of bad experiences with balloons, the worst example I could possibly come up with is if the balloon is losing helium, and midway through the evening you're starting to see the balloons look a little droopy. Depending on when that happens, if it's at the end of the night it's probably not as big of a deal as it is when guests are walking into the ballroom.

"I've never had a situation where something popped and scared somebody. In fact, in most cases people are wanting to take them home, and if that's the case then by and large, if you think about a traditional centerpiece that's a floral centerpiece, sometimes you don't want guests to take those home, because the base itself might have been rented from the florist.

"You usually are using a balloon once, so giving those to the guests is not as big of a deal as making sure they don't walk out with some centerpiece container that you have to return to the florist the next day. So loss of helium I guess would be the worst situation I've seen happen with balloons.

"Here is another way that balloons are used, which is not a direct way to make money, but it helps them make money in an indirect way. Sometimes we will do an activity at an auction called a balloon pop, which is more or less when a group is purchasing a balloon for a flat rate. $25 is pretty typical, and they're popping the balloon, and inside the balloon is some gift card to a local establishment, that usually the value of it is $10-$20, or it may even be more.

Photo and Balloons by Sandi Masori

"If they had a $20 gift card to Starbucks, for instance, and they put that in the silent auction section, they might just get $15 for that, but if they're able to put it in a balloon and conceal what it is, and charge $25, And say, 'by the way you might get $100 to Ruth's Chris Steak-house in here.' Because one of them might hold something that's more desirable than just $25, then the non-profit is able to maximize the value on those lower valued items.

"So in that case it's helping the client make more money because of the way that it's being used. I forget all the marketing triggers as to why someone will buy something. Sometimes you buy something with the idea that you're going to make more money, sometimes it's to save more money in the long term, sometimes it's that you're going to look cool to your friends.

"I think that perhaps when I visit with my clients oftentimes they're looking at the standpoint of affordability, so it may be more tied into that, creating a different experience that's affordable that absolutely impacts their bottom line when it comes down to their net.

Photo and Design by Anne McGovern

"As for themes, '80s are coming back pretty strong, and Gatsby. I think Gatsby because of the movie. The other thing is Tiffany's just launched a whole Gatsby line of jewelry, which I'm going to be blogging about at some point too, because I know that will generate more interest in a Gatsby theme. That's an incredibly popular theme right now. The other one that I see is 'back to the '80s' events. All those people who graduated in the '80s are now the ones who are now planning auctions, and so they're like 'let's do back to the '80s', so I've seen varying degrees of involvement with a 'back to '80s' theme. And then the one that is, really popular is Italy, and specifically, Venice.

"Italy is a big place to go to; people like to go to Italy, and specifically, Venice, because it tends to focus around the masks, Carnival. Now that said, it's an expensive theme, or can be, to pull off. Sometimes when people are doing these themes, they are going towards this whole concept of creating the location within their gymnasium, or creating it within their hotel venue. So if you're trying to recreate Italy, or Venice, with its water, it takes a lot to create that.

Photo and Design by Jill Shortreed

Photo and Design by Joette Giardina

"In comparison, let's say you go with the white gala, right? That's what your theme is, the white gala. Well, white is a pretty easy theme to go with. You can do a lot, and get a lot of white balloons; you can have people dress in white; you can have white napkins with off-white tablecloths. You can do a lot more with it much easier than trying to recreate Greece or Venice or Brazil in your auction.

"In fact I did a webinar a couple of months ago talking about creative auction themes and we go through a lot of photos from different auctions. I break out into eight different categories the themes that are out there, and your location themes are the most expensive to pull off.

"There was one time where I was at an auction, and I used the balloons that they had there to direct people to certain areas. I took a cluster of balloons, and I am walking around and saying 'follow me down to the ballroom area,' because we needed to have something visual to get guests attention, and that was the easiest way because it could get above the height of the guests to direct them to something. I guess you could say it's marketing; it's navigation- A useful

Photo and Design by Sandi Masori

tool, it's your GPS in that case. So I've seen it used in that way too. It's easy, I just tied them on my wrist, it's not something cumbersome. I could probably put it on, well I wasn't wearing a belt, but you could probably put it on a belt and do the same sort of thing."

Chris also had some ideas on how to use balloons for maximum profit.

Chris: "Everybody's main objective is to raise money for their charity, but the people that go to these galas, a lot of them they go to galas maybe four or five times a year, different galas, and everybody understands that they're there to try to raise money for the charity, but they also want to have a good time. They want it to be exciting.

"So you have to really go above and beyond, and really make this event look spectacular and 'wow' on the limited budget that you have. Balloons are just a great way of doing that. The volume you can get with balloons is tremendous. So I try to show them that, 'yes, you're trying to make money, but look what you can get, and look what a difference it's going to make between your event and somebody else's event, and the guests that go there now will say, wow. This was great; I'm certainly going to come back next year; it was fun.'

"Usually, for some reason they're stuck on their own centerpiece, they like to get a little floral piece; maybe that's just what they're used to. So that just covers table, so in order to fill up the space in the room we're always suggesting suspending large balloon creations from the ceiling. They can see that just the volume of big three foot round balloon alone is a 'wow.' Then when we start showing them the embellishments, and the different chandeliers that can be hung throughout the room, and how many they can get, maybe 20 or 30 arrangements throughout the room, suspended up high, nothing on the ground that gets covered up by the large crowds that they have. They seem to really like that, all the décor up high off the ground.

"We try to always wow them at the entrance, make a great first impression, and then next thing is filling the vast open space above, hanging from the ceiling. Then if they've got budgets, then we start trying to incorporate centerpieces or perimeter décor around the room.

"At all these events there's always an announcement. There's always a revealing; they like to say how much they've raised, or what they did in the past year, so they like to make a big announcement. We're always suggesting some kind of a balloon drop during that time, or streamer launchers or confetti launchers. So they'll go with handheld streamer launchers that they'll shoot off during the announcement. Then after the announcement it's usually the party stuff, the band gets a little louder; they play different kinds of music, the fun is starting to happen."

Photo and Design by Chris Potts

Blenda's non-profit work tends to be based more around races and runs. Here's what she has to say about that...

Blenda: "A lot of our nonprofit work are races and runs. If that's the event that they're producing, I would definitely tell them to decorate the finish, start or finish line arch. It's easy to brand their nonprofit with balloons, because it's easy to bring that color in. No matter where it is, or what the event is, you can add their brand to the event with balloons.

"We recently did one, for our local YMCA. It was an event production company that did it, and it was basically just hors d'oeuvres. It was a rally for their supporters and their board, and they led their guests into this venue, and they led them through black pipe and drape with occasionally a colored sign, and at the end of this pipe and drape was a balloon rainbow.

"They were showing how it was adding color to the event, so it was really kind of neat. We were able to provide them with a tunnel of balloons that represented a rainbow, and it was an easy way for them to bring the guests in, and it was kind of interactive. They went through the rainbow, and then they were in the venue where the event was taking place.

"We will be working with the American Heart Association, and they like to do a village, and their villages are colored. They've got red, green, and yellow, and we will use large flying balloons, and then balloons inside each village that will represent each village; one is community, one is health, etc. They've done this for years, using balloons to differentiate between the different villages."

Photo and Design by Blenda Berrier

Blenda also mentioned tents, "we'll decorate tents with stage décor, because they're usually speaking. American Cancer Society usually has a stage, because they do a lot of long walks, and they're relays where they'll have a stage, so we'll usually do some stage décor, some columns. Those are going to be out there for a long period of time. You want to make sure they're weighted correctly. Sculptures are another thing that are really popular."

Photo and Design by Blenda Berrier

Photo and Design by Sandi Masori

Photo and Design by Sandi Masori

Photo and Design by Sandi Masori

Homecoming

Homecomings are another type of event that easily lends itself to balloons. Blenda finds herself decorating a lot of them and had this to share with us...

Photo and Design by Blenda Berrier

Blenda: "I do a lot of work with schools. I do a lot of homecomings, and lot of proms. I think the Homecoming dances here in Florida have become just as big as Prom. They're really using the venues; you're using the stadiums. I had one this year that used their school to have their dance, all of the rest of them are using large spaces, the stadium, hotel ballrooms, for their events. As far as trends go, I would say that Homecoming is becoming just as large as Prom.

"We generally do entrance and dance floor décor for most of them; that's where we'll start. This year we have a school that's doing a small balloon release after the court's announced. As for themes, it's 50/50, some of the school's are using themes for their Homecoming dances, and then the other ones are using their school colors.

"One of the themes that we're seeing this year is lights; they're just doing lights. Another one is 'a Salute to our Heroes,' and they're doing a mix of superheroes as well as military, police, and firemen. That was kind of different, I had never even seen that theme before. Under the sea is a pretty traditional one. Hollywood, red carpet is definitely a popular one.

'When we're planning the décor, sometimes I meet with the kids, and sometimes I only meet with the advisor. Once in a while the kids will say 'we don't want balloons.' But the advisor would say 'just wait and talk to her, and see what she has to offer, and maybe you'll change your mind.'

"And then I come in and meet with them, and they're like 'wow; we didn't know that you could do that.' Meeting with these sophomores and juniors in high school, and they weren't really sure what to expect, but they're always blown away and happy when it's finished.

"Generally I know their theme, so I come prepared with photographs that are going to best represent their theme. Nowadays it's digital pictures; I'll use my computer or iPad, I still have my traditional portfolio that I'll bring and let them look through, but most of the presentations are digital these days."

Photo and Design by Blenda Berrier

Summary

You've seen some pictures of amazing events, running the gamut from whimsical to very up-scale. You've seen some of the range of options. This is by no means an exhaustive list. There is so much that can be done with balloons, the possibilities are literally limitless.

The real take-away that I want you to get is that if you approach your balloon artist as a partner, in the very beginning of the planning process, and share with them the vision and the approximate budget, then you'll likely be very pleasantly surprised at what they'll come up with- most likely incredible designs that you wouldn't have thought about on your own. The more that you collaborate with your balloon professional on your events, the more that you'll see that your range of options and offerings expands. You'll be able to have an entire new range of things to offer your clients, winning you their admiration and repeat business. And once you find that special balloon artist, the one that works well with you, and gets the vision that you are trying to sell, stop shopping around and work with them exclu-

Photo and Design by Jill Shortreed

sively. They can probably create custom packages to meet your budgets, and the stronger your relationship, the more new and novel pieces you'll be able to offer your clients.

So, the moral of the story is don't write off balloons thinking that your event is too high-end. Instead, collaborate with your balloon artist and you will be shocked at what you can do together.

Photo and Design by Steve Jones

Design by Steve Jones

Photo and Design by Chris Potts

Photo and Design by Anne McGovern

Photo and Design by Blenda Berrier

Photo and Design by Dianna Glandon

Photo and Design by Holland and Sean Muscio

Photo and Design by Jill Shortreed

Photo and Design by Joette Giardina

Photo and Design by Sandi Masori

Photo and Design by Steve Jones

Photo and Design by Tammy Corzine

Photo and Design by Sandi Masori

Photo and Design by Dianna Glandon

Appendix
Glossary

260- Long skinny balloon that best known for being made into hats and animals by balloon entertainers. So named because when it's fully inflated it's approximately 2 inches wide and 60 inches long.

350- Long skinny balloon that is thicker than the traditional 260 balloon. So named because when it's fully inflated it's approximately 3 inches wide and 50 inches long.

Air-filled décor- Décor that utilizes air or nitrogen instead of helium. This décor will not float, but using framing and various techniques will last much longer than helium filled décor and is infinitely more versatile.

Anagram- One of the main manufacturers of decorator quality foil balloons, they have been gaining ground in the decorator market lately with their innovative foil shapes.

Awesome Bouquets- A style of balloon bouquet that uses non-round balloons and has a different shape than the round balloon bouquets. They are very elegant looking and make great buffet pieces or ambiance décor if put on top of a pedestal. They're a little too bulky to use as table centerpieces.

Awesome Column – A column that is based on the awesome bouquet. They have the same sort of top and spread using non-round balloons. There are smaller balloons in the stand part of the column, and a light in the bottom so that the small balloons give off a gentle illumination effect.

Balloon Arches- The most well-known form of balloon décor next to the balloons on string. Arches can be framed or unframed, and be made in a variety of patterns and shapes. The most well known is the spiral arch, though it's not necessarily always the best choice for the space.

Balloon Bouquets – This is a group of helium filled balloons arranged and tied to a weight of some sort.

Balloon Column Lamps – (Lighted Balloon) - these are really elegant and elicit a *"Wow"* response- this refers to balloon columns that have a balloon on top (often a jumbo balloon) that has a light bulb inside of the top balloon. The light can be a soft light, all the way to a bright bulb with a 100 watt output. Your balloon professional will know which lights work best without getting too hot.

Balloon Columns – Free standing balloon structure where groups of balloons are set directly on top of each other in various ways. There are many different shapes and patterns that the column could have, though the most widely known is the spiral pattern.

Balloon Curls- (also called balloon squiggles or balloon spirals) A 260 balloon that has been inflated into a spiral or squiggle shape.

Balloon Drop- This is also a pretty well known use for balloons, often seen on New Year's Eve or at political conventions. There is a bag of balloons on the ceiling, and at a given cue, a cord is pulled releasing all the balloons inside.

Balloon Release- This is like a balloon drop, but in the opposite direction- the bag may be at ground level, and when the cord is pulled, the balloons will float up to the ceiling or into the air. Please note that if you are doing a balloon release outdoors, you should check your local ordinances and notify the FAA to make sure that the balloons are not in a flight path.

Balloon Trees- often used by those out of the industry to mean "balloon bouquet", to a professional decorator this is probably going to be taken as an actual tree made from balloons- like a palm tree or an apple tree.

Balloon Wall- A wall made out of balloons. It can be made with a hard structure, like a steel grid, or made from a series of garland that is put together.

Betallic- One of the main manufacturers of decorator quality balloons.

Brazilian Technique – a packing technique popularized by Brazilian balloon artists. This technique allows the balloon artist to cover large or wide columns or support beams with balloons.

California Balloon Laws – these are laws in California that govern how mylar, or foil balloons are used. The main points of the law is that every foil balloon should be individually tied to an anchor, that they shouldn't be grouped together, and that nothing that conducts electricity should be attached to a balloon that is filled with a gas that is lighter than air (helium for example). Even though at present only California has these laws, it is considered best practices to abide by them in any state.

CBA – Certified Balloon Artist – this is a certification awarded after an intensive set of written and practical exams

Classic Décor – This is simple lines and colors- arches, swags and columns. This type of décor is really effective for adding ambiance or covering large spaces.

Cloud 9 – (Fantasy Cloud)- This is a really popular design that featured 2 quads of balloons stacked on top of each other and a larger balloon at the top. It's called a cloud 9 because it uses 9 balloons. Often it's used with tulle behind a head table in series of 5, or individually filled with helium and having wide ribbons hanging down, or air-filled on top of a base plate and pole. Very effective décor for outdoors because of its single anchor point.

Column Based Sculpture- this style of balloon sculpture is based on a single baseplate and pole, and uses a technique of varying the balloon size to create the sculpture. Some examples of this type of sculpture would be a carrot or a Nut-cracker guy.

Criss-Cross Canopy- Often used as a dance floor treatment, it is characterized by having two arches (usually string of pearls) that crisscross each other across the middle.

Deco-twisting – This is industry jargon referring to a decorator who brings non-round (or long skinny balloon) elements into their décor. Using the blend of techniques, a balloon pro can get incredible detail and lines added to their décor.

Duplet – Two balloons tied together, a basic building block of balloon décor

Exploding Balloons- this is a great alternative to the traditional balloon drop. Usually these are jumbo balloons (3') stuffed with 150- 200 smaller balloons (5" balloons). When the outer balloon is exploded, the little balloons fall down on the crowd. Often this will lead to an impromptu "balloon stomp" from even the most sophisticated of audiences. There are many methods to do exploding balloons, some using pyrotechnic techniques, some using electricity and others manually exploded. The cool thing about exploding balloons is that unlike a balloon drop, they are taken for-granted as part of the décor until the big reveal.

Fantasy Cloud – Another way to describe Cloud 9's

Fantasy Flowers- refers to the practice of making flowers out of un-inflated balloons, often with wires inside each balloon. Using this technique, incredibly real looking flowers can be created that will last much longer than live florals

Fantasy People- This uses the same technique as fantasy flowers, only instead of creating flowers, small people sculptures are created. Each fantasy person could be up to the size of a Barbie doll.

Float Time- The length of time that a helium filled balloon will float. Depending on the brand, this could be from 6- 20 hours for an 11" balloon. If it's treated with Hi-float this can be increased dramatically.

Foil Balloons- the correct term for what is more popularly referred to as "mylar" balloons. The term "mylar" actually belongs to the DuPont company, and they haven't used it to make balloons for a very long time. Many people, balloon professionals included, still use the generic term "mylar" in place of "foil balloons". (I am guilty of this myself more often than not).

Garland – A string of balloons made by packing groups of balloons on top of each other. Can be made with air or helium. Garland that is un-framed and air-filled will hang, helium filled garland will form an arch.

Herringbone Arch – (Fishbone Arch) An arch that starts out as a string of pearls arch, with a single line of balloons, and then duplets are added between each balloon, giving it a herringbone, or fishbone look. The bottom is flat, but the top is full.

Hi-float- this is an additive that can be put inside of a balloon to extend its float time. It's similar to Elmer's glue in that it is a non toxic polymer gel. It seals the pores of the balloon, thereby keeping the helium inside for a longer period of time. It can extend the float time of an 11" balloon from 18 hours to a couple of weeks. It's not recommended for outdoor use though as it does not do well with changes in weather or humidity.

Lighted Balloons – Another way to call Balloon Lamps

Link-O-Loon Canopy- A canopy using the linking balloons, often done in a cross hatch pattern.

Link-O-Loons – A type of balloon that have an extra tail on the end so that they can be tied together in chains. There are a couple of manufacturers who make these balloons, but Betallic was the first one to come out with it, and so got the first to market advantage. By force of habit, many balloon artists will use the phrase "link-o-loons" regardless of what brand they are using.

Megaloons – Large foil balloons in the shape of numbers and letters. This is a brand name, but here too they had a first to market advantage, and the term is often used even when other brands are being used.

Open Canopy- Often used as a dance floor treatment, it is characterized by having 4 columns around the dance floor, and string of pearl arches jumping from one arch to the next.

Party Ball- (Topiary Ball) ball made from 8-12 round balloons that can either be filled with helium and floated, or air-filled and hung.

Precision Wall- A balloon wall made from a series of garland that has been connected together.

Quad – Two duplets twisted together, most arches, columns and garlands are based on quads stacked together.

Qualatex- One of the main manufacturers of decorator quality balloons

Quick Links- A type of balloon that have an extra tail on the end so that they can be tied together in chains. The "Quick Link" balloon is by Qualatex, but since they came out a few years after "Link-O-Loons", many balloon artists will use that term regardless of which brand they are using.

RMS- a framing system using a flexible plastic matrix. They can be cut into many shapes for easy framing of shapes. It's named after its inventor. The full name is Rouse Matrix System, but everyone calls it RMS.

Roman Columns – (Sculpted/Princess Columns) - Balloon columns where the top and bottom layers of balloons have a wider girth than the center layers of balloons- lending a Greek or Roman column look to the design. This design looks much more elegant that it's standard balloon column cousin.

Round vs. Non Round Balloons – Industry jargon referring to either the round balloons that most people are used to seeing in arches or floating and the long skinny balloons often used by clowns or balloon entertainers. There is a growing trend in the industry to combine both types of balloons for a unique look, more detail, and to create different types of lines.

Sculpted/Princess Columns- Some artists use this phrase to refer to Roman Columns.

Sculptures- This is where balloon professionals really get to "Wow" and strut their stuff. A sculpture could be a simple twisted creation or an elaborate 3-d topiary design. Using a variety of techniques, a good balloon artist can get an almost exact likeness of any mascot or logo.

SDS- A grid system that can be used to make columns, arches and walls. Named after its inventor, the full name is Skistimas Design System, but everyone calls it SDS

Spiral Arch- A balloon arch with a spiral pattern made from the balloons. It has a lot of energy and is especially good if you want to lead the eye up one side and down the other- like over promotional aisles in a store for example.

Spiral garland- Industry term describing the way that the garland is packed, more than the pattern being used. In this style, groups of balloons are stacked on top of each other, and can easily form a spiral pattern. Other patterns like zig-zag, arrows, zipper, flowers, diamonds, color chunks, or even solid colors are possible.

Spiral Topiary- A centerpiece style that uses a metal frame that goes around and around in a spiral pattern. They are very tall and elegant, but have a lot of rhythm and negative space.

Stacker- Industry jargon term for a balloon decorator that only uses round balloons- so named because many of the décor pieces that they create are made by "stacking" groups of balloons together.

String of Pearls Arch- A line of balloons where you see the full balloon next to another full balloon, next to another. It's not as full as a spiral arch. Can be a bit more elegant than the traditional spiral arch.

String of Pearls Canopy- Often used as a dance floor treatment, or as a Chuppah, or as a focal point area, it is characterized by having a series of string of pearl arches that are so close together that it looks as though it's a solid canopy. The key to this type of canopy is to have a lot of weight at the bottom to account for the extra torque that is put on the poles holding it up.

Topiary Design- (Party Ball)- this term could refer to two different things, one is a ball made from 8-12 round balloons that can either be filled with helium and floated, or air-filled and hung. The other way it is used is to describe the 3-d sculptures that are built around a metal form- much like the plant topiaries that you might see at Disneyland.

Tuf-Tex- Manufacturer of balloons that are often used outdoors. Most decorators will use Qualatex or Betallic indoors, but often will choose Tuf- Tex for their outdoor events.

Tunnel- A 3-dimensional structure that people can walk through- often used at the entrance to a room. A tunnel can be made from a series of arches- either string of pearl, or garland arches. Other popular ways to make tunnels are with linking balloons or RMS.

Twisted balloons- Industry jargon describing shapes and figures made from the long skinny balloons that need to be twisted together.

Twister- Industry term for a person that makes figures and shapes out of the long skinny balloons- usually as a form of entertainment. They are called "twisters" because they twist balloons together to form those shapes and sculptures.

Weaving- A technique using the long skinny balloons to create a balloon fabric. This technique can be used for sculptures, and wearable balloon fashions. It is exactly as it sounds, where the balloons are woven together in a variety of fashions.

Photo and Design by Joette Giardina

Photo and Design by Anne McGovern

Photo and Design by Blenda Berrier

233

Photo and Design by Holland and Sean Muscio

Photo and Design by Sandi Masori

Photo and Design by Sandi Masori

Photo and Design by Tammy Corzine

Photo and Design by Tammy Corzine

Directory

Anne McGovern, CBA

Elegant Balloons

http://www.elegant-balloons.com

Pearl River, NY

(845) 323-8851

After spending 20 years in the corporate meetings and events industry with Goldman Sachs and Avon, Anne took time off to raise her children. She started a home-based event planning business in 2005; and after exposure to the world of balloon decorating, realized this was where her skills and passion lay.

Anne opened Elegant Balloons in 2007, focusing on high-quality, unique balloon decor. Anne's first convention was FLOAT 2009, where she became a CBA (Certified Balloon Artist). Since then, she has attended many educational seminars, including FLOAT & World Balloon Convention (WBC), where she won numerous awards. Anne will be teaching two classes at World Balloon Convention 2014 in Denver. Her work has been featured in "Images Magazine" *(a balloon industry publication)* along with other publications.

She loves creating and sharing her ideas for sellable, long-lasting balloon decor with pizzazz and twisted accents. Today, Anne operates a successful home-based balloon company in the New York/New Jersey area and is known throughout the industry for creating breathtaking centerpiece displays.

Blenda Berrier, CBA

Balloon and Event Construction Company

http://www.balloonandevents.com

Jacksonville, Florida

(904) 220-5411

After being introduced to the world of balloon decorating in 2001, Blenda loved the creative possibilities of working with the art medium of balloons. Thus, she immediately attended the International Balloon Arts Convention (IBAC) in Chicago where she took numerous classes and continued to attend the IBAC for the next several years. After much work and study, she received her Certified Balloon Artist (CBA) certification.

Over the years, Blenda has enjoyed working the long hours and days it has taken to grow The Balloon Construction Company into a successful event decor company. She is proud of the extensive list of corporate clients that have trusted us with their events, including a 10,000 balloon release for the Jacksonville Jaguars.

As a Jacksonville native and mother to two boys and married 17 years, she absolutely loves living on the First Coast.

Chris Potts, CBA

Balloon Masters

http://www.balloonmasters.net

Buffalo, New York

(716) 685-5590

Chris Potts, Co-Owner & lead designer of Balloon Masters, a full service decorating company, is an expert in creating amazing balloon décor. Chris & his wife opened their first location in 1992 specializing in retail balloon gifts for the holidays. At the time, they intrigued clients at their store and satellite mall and shopping center locations when they put gifts and fresh flowers inside various sizes of latex balloons.

Soon after Chris became a Certified Balloon Artist, he opened a second location and a design studio where he began designing incredible balloon décor for all of Western New York. Starting with theme décor for Mitzvah events, weddings and numerous school functions, Chris honed his skills and quickly became a top balloon decorator for corporate functions. He has developed a team to decorate locally while he travels the country setting up trade shows, rock concerts and other corporate events.

Besides being honored as an instructor at some of the nation's largest balloon decorating conventions, Chris has won numerous decorating awards in mural competitions and won consecutive awards in manufacturer decorating contests as well as special recognition for innovation and technique.

Chris is a charter member of 'Your Balloon Pros' and brings his energetic personality, enthusiasm to travel, and expertise in the rigging challenges of large venues and outdoor events to this amazing team of event decorators.

Dianna Glandon, CBA

Above the Rest Balloon and Event Designs

http://www.aboveresteventdesigns.com

Knoxville, Tennessee

(865) 719-8110

Dianna Glandon is President and founder of Above the Rest Balloon and Event Designs. She is a former teacher and Student Council Advisor who planned numerous small and large-scale events for over 15 years, often using balloons to create excitement and motivation at those events. Upon discovering the exciting, magical power that quality balloon décor can bring to any event, Above the Rest Balloon & Event Designs was born in 2006. She absolutely loves creating unique décor for people planning special events and celebrations. 'It is a blessing to serve those people saving them time, energy; stress and money, while making their event look Above the Rest and make them exclaim, 'WOW!'"

Glandon has studied with the best instructors in the balloon event decorating industry from around the world, including instructors from Japan, Italy, Australia, England, Belgium, Italy, Netherlands, France, and the United States. She has traveled throughout the US, learning and forming relationships with design masters and is now considered an expert in the balloon industry, staying abreast of the most recent trends, designs, and products. She became a CBA (Certified Balloon Artist) in 2010, designating her as a high-quality balloon professional and one of 3,000 CBA's in the world. At Ballooniversity 2012, Dianna taught two classes to fellow artists to share some of the knowledge she has learned.

Holland & Sean Muscio

Balloonacy Atlanta

http://balloonacyatlanta.com

Atlanta, Georgia

(404) 351-0538

A graduate of Meredith College in Raleigh, Holland brings her love of the art of celebration' to every event she designs. Her experience dates back as far as elementary school when she began decorating with flowers. She worked for years in the arts and ticketing industries before becoming a floral designer, balloon artist, and entrepreneur and has been producing events or event decor for over 25 years.

Sean served in the Navy. Then, after holding jobs in the IT and construction industries, he was searching for a way to be self-employed when he joined forces with wife & partner, Holland, to purchase Balloonacy from its original owner. Sean uses the talents and skills he grew in his previous jobs to become the company's go-to operations guy.

Balloonacy, owned by Holland & Sean Muscio since 2005, has been providing the Metro Atlanta area with unique balloon décor for almost 30 years. The company has decorated events ranging from first birthday parties, to Grand Openings, to corporate events surrounding the 1996 Centennial Olympic Games, Bar & Bat Mitzvahs, Fun Runs & Walks and just about every one of life's celebrations in between! Together, Holland and Sean strive to produce quality events for their clients. In addition to balloon décor, the company also provides themed centerpieces, props, flowers and more for their clients to enjoy.

Jill Shortreed, CBA

Charleston Balloon Company, LLC

http://www.charlestonballooncompany.com

Mount Pleasant, South Carolina

(843) 856-9121

Jill Shortreed, Principal Partner and Senior Designer of Charleston Balloon Company, has been designing exceptional and affordable balloon and event décor for corporate, civic and social events for over 20 years.

She has designed and decorated incredible events up and down the East Coast from first birthday parties in New York City to Bruce Springsteen's Album release at The Stone Pony, along countless large scale Corporate and Non-profit events.

Jill has incredible vision and has become a top balloon decorator for corporate and large scale functions in the Carolina Region. She is the creative force behind Charleston Balloon Company's success. Having a background in marketing and finance, she is able to take your event and make it center stage while staying on budget. Jill is an award-winning artist. Her designs have been featured on TV and selected to appear in trade publications and International websites/blogs, including 'Party and Paper Magazine', 'Images Magazine' and 'Qualatex.com'.

As co-owner of Charleston Balloon Company, Scott Shortreed, CBA, has vast knowledge of mechanics and design which enables him to build and install decor that seems to magically appear. Scott is a graduate of Johnson and Wales University and has served in the hospitality industry for over 30 years. Charleston Balloon is one of only two companies in South Carolina to have two CBA's on staff.

The philosophy behind Charleston Balloon is to design creative, affordable, eco-friendly décor using quality supplies, while upholding an exceptional reputation to always strive to exceed the client's expectations. Charleston Balloon Company is fully dedicated to safe, green environmental business practices and event recycling.

Joette Giardina, CBA

Party People Celebration Company

http://partypeoplecelebrationco.com

Lakeland, Florida

(863) 255-2025

Before Joette Giardina, became owner of Party People Celebration Company in 2003, she started creating balloon decor for friends, church groups, and family. She then expanded her business as the new owner of Party People Celebration Company. She has success-fully grown her business by providing professional, caring service to her clients. Based in Lakeland, Florida, Party People Celebration Company also serves Orlando and Tampa. Joette strives to meet the needs of individuals, families, small businesses, corporations, and non-profit organizations to create memorable events.

In addition to decor, Joette also offers full service event coordination for your special event. Since February 2010, Joette has won the bid to coordinate the décor for the Lakeland Chamber Annual Dinner, at which 1,000 Lakeland business leaders attend. For ten years, families planning their son's or daughter's Bar/Bat Mitzvah events, have re-laxed instead of stressed, as Joette worked on pre-planning, coordi-nation of vendors and day of coordination services.

Through on-going balloon industry training, Joette learns from top designers which enables her to provide clients with the latest tech-niques and products that add the WOW factor to their events! In 2010 & 2013, she was honored to be an instructor at 'FLOAT,' an inter-national balloon convention.

At the 2012 World Balloon Convention, Joette served on the U.S. Me-dium Sculpture team helping create 'Springtime in the Smokies' *(de-signed by Rachel Glandon of Above the Rest Balloons, Knoxville TN)* The team was the ONLY U.S. competitor out of 144 international entrants to place in the 2012 World Balloon Convention. In October 2008, Joette was a member of the International balloon team for the AEMI Balloon Couture Fashion show in Shanghai, China.

Steven Jones

Balloon Designers

http://www.balloondesigners.com

Seattle, Washington

(206) 450-5088

It all began in 1996 in Cincinnati, Ohio, at a "start your own business" expo with the purchase of a balloon stuffing machine. Shortly after, Steven realized putting gifts inside balloons would not create the financial stability he desired, he expanded his business into the world of balloon decorating.

Since then, Steven has become known in the balloon decorating and entertaining world as an award-winning designer, respected instructor, and industry producer. He has been a regular columnist on BalloonHQ.com, the industry's largest support website, and served three years on the advisory board for Betallic, Inc., one of the industry's largest manufacturers of foil balloons.

Steven has won over 20 industry and event awards, including 'Best of Show' booth designs and the balloon industry's esteemed 'Designer of the Year' award. In 2011, Chance Fashion Group in Seattle recognized Steven for outstanding efforts in balloon couture designs. This was the first time his work had received an award from an organization outside the event industry, making it a very special honor.

His efforts have been showcased in such industry magazines as 'Balloon Images', 'Balloons & Parties Magazine', 'Party & Paper Magazine' and 'Florists' Review.' While in Shanghai, China, in 2007, photos of his balloon outfits were showcased internationally in newspapers, periodicals, magazines and news broadcasts.

Steven graduated Summa Cum Laude with a degree in audio/video production and formed AeraDeco Video. He has directed, edited, and produced over 60 different full-length instructional videos aimed at educating the professional balloon decorator and entertainer. Currently, Steven works with a dozen balloon artists from around the world to create top-quality educational videos.

In 2008, his emphasis on education expanded when he produced the FLOAT Convention. FLOAT provides top quality education for balloon professionals who desire to improve their career. FLOAT has become recognized in the balloon decorating industry as THE convention to attend if one is dedicated to building a successful balloon decor business.

Steven relocated his business to Seattle, WA in 2010, where he became the founding member of the Puget Sound Balloon Network, a trade association of regional balloon professionals. Steven also serves as a board member of the Seattle ISES chapter.

Photo and Design by Steve Jones

Tammy Corzine

Celebrations

http://celebrationsohio.com

Delphos, Ohio

(Service area – Northwest & West Central Ohio)

(419) 695-4455

Tammy Corzine is the Owner and Lead Designer at 'Celebrations'. She has been working in the balloon and special event industry since 1990. In 1994 she started her own home-based decorating business and in 2004 made the move to a storefront and expanded into retail balloons and party supplies. Since then her business has continued to thrive and grow including a move to a larger storefront in 2009. 'Celebrations' now provides decor for any type of event including private, corporate and non-profit events. Tammy specializes in creating unique, large scale balloon decor and enjoys the challenge of 'wow-ing' clients and guests with balloons.

She has contributed to multiple articles and has been quoted in 'Images Magazine' and 'Party & Paper Retailer Magazine'. She attends various educational seminars and conventions throughout the year to make sure she has all the most up to date options and ideas for her clients.

Tammy is a graduate of Lincolnview High School and Vantage Vocational School and went on to receive an associate's degree in Marketing and Business Administration from the University of Northwestern Ohio.

'Celebrations' is proud to sponsor decor for various events in their community.

Photo and Design by Sandi Masori

Photo and Design by Sandi Masori

To See Complete Video Interviews:
Go to BalloonUtopia.com/EPG

To Get in touch with Sandi
www.BalloonUtopia.com

To See Sandi's Media Appearances
www.BalloonUtopia.com/media

To Book Sandi/ Balloon Utopia for an event
Sandi@balloonutopia.com
619 339 8024

To Get Full- Color PDF of This Book Go To
www.BalloonUtopia.com/colorEPG

Photo and Design by Sandi Masori

Made in the USA
San Bernardino, CA
22 July 2015